Delton T. Horn's
All-Time Favorite
Electronic Projects

Delton T. Horn's
All-Time Favorite
Electronic Projects

Delton T. Horn

TAB BOOKS Inc.
Blue Ridge Summit, PA

FIRST EDITION
FIRST PRINTING

Library of Congress Cataloging in Publication Data

Horn, Delton T.
    [All-time favorite electronic projects]
    Delton T. Horn's all-time favorite electronic projects / by Delton
T. Horn.
        p.   cm.
    Includes index.
    ISBN 0-8306-3105-4 (pbk.)
    1. Electronic—Amateurs manuals.   I. Title.   II. Title: All-
time favorite electronic projects.
TK9965.H639   1988
621.381—dc19   88-19112
                                                         CIP

TAB BOOKS Inc. offers software for sale. For information and a catalog, please
contact TAB Software Department, Blue Ridge Summit, PA 17294-0850.

Questions regarding the content of this book
should be addressed to:

    Reader Inquiry Branch
    TAB BOOKS Inc.
    Blue Ridge Summit, PA 17294-0214

Contents

Editor's Preface

Delton Horn has been an electronics experimenter for over 18 years and has worked in a variety of fields as an electronics technician. He is now occupied as a full-time technical author. All 16 of these projects were extracted from six of his best projects books currently published by TAB. These books are: *117 Practical IC Projects You Can Build* (TAB book #2645), *Using Integrated Circuit Logic Devices* (TAB book #1645), *Amplifiers Simplified* (TAB book #2885), *Transistor Circuit Design with Experiments* (TAB book #1875), *How to Design Op Amp Circuits with Projects & Experiments* (TAB book #1765), and *Designing IC Circuits* (TAB book #1925). Numerous other titles covering all aspects of electronics are available from TAB. Also available is a new line of electronics engineering and design titles by Mr. Horn and by many other authors.

The variety of projects in this book will appeal to both the beginner and the more experienced electronic hobbyist. However, the emphasis is on practicality. This text is divided into two parts. Part I is For the Home. Included are gadgets like setting up an intercom or building your own digital clock. Also contained in this section are projects you can construct to create or build upon audio equipment, such as amplifiers and tone controls.

Part II discusses items For the Shop. Described are a variety of circuits and testing devices to use in your electronics hobby shop, such as a digital capacitance meter or a multiple-output power supply. When completed and added to your current equipment, these handy devices will make your shop an easier and more enjoyable place to work.

It is sincerely hoped you will enjoy these projects while simultaneously learning and producing a useful, working item for your home or shop.

PART I:

For the Home

PROJECT 1:
Intercom

The TCA830S is a powerful, inexpensive op amp IC that makes it a particularly attractive choice for intercoms because the circuit can be built with a minimum number of components. Many other op amps do not produce the power required for loudspeaker operation without the addition of a further stage of transistor amplification. The basic circuit is contained at the main station while the distant station merely comprises a loudspeaker and a calling switch. The two stations are connected by a 3-wire flex.

The circuit is shown in Fig. 1-1. The TCA830S requires a heatsink and is fitted with tabs. A printed circuit is recommended, incorporating two l-inch (25 mm) squares of copper to which the IC tabs can be soldered for the heatsink. Component positioning is not critical because the circuit handles only audio frequencies.

The transformer (T) has a 50:1 turns ratio and is used as a step-down transformer between the IC and speaker(s); it also works as a step-up transformer between the speakers and IC in the reverse mode. In other words, the transformer coil with the larger number of turns is connected to pin 8 on the IC. Instead of purchasing this transformer ready-made, it can be wound on a stack of standard transformer core laminates 0.35 mm thick, giving a core cross-section of 22.5 mm². Windings are 600 turns of 0.2 mm (36 s.w.g.) and 300 turns of 0.06 mm (46 s.w.g.) enameled copper wire.

The purpose of the transformer is to enable standard 4Ω to 16Ω loudspeakers to be used both as microphones and speakers. These

1

Table 1-1. Parts List for Project 1: Intercom.

IC	TCA8305 op amp
R1	20KΩ(remote station)
R2	29 Ω
C1	100μF, electrolytic, 3V
C2	0.1μF
C3	1000μF, electrolytic, 12V
T	50:1 turns ratio, 5W
SPKRS	4Ω(preferred)
S1	press break/make switch
S2	press make/break switch

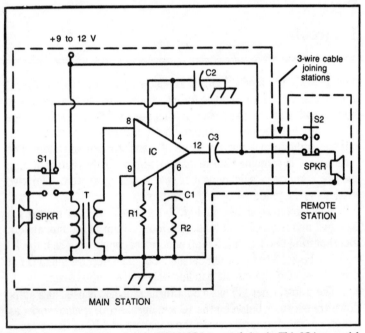

Fig. 1-1. Intercom circuit using the TCA830S integrated circuit. This IC is powerful enough to operate fairly large loudspeakers. Component values are given in the text.

speakers can be of any size, bearing in mind that the maximum power output of the circuit is of the order of 2 watts on a 12-volt supply. The intercom circuit will work on any battery voltage down to 6 volts, 9 or 12 volts being recommended for general operation.

PROJECT 2:
Car Thief Alarm

This circuit is by Siemens and is based around their TDB0556A dual timer IC. See Fig. 2-1. The first timing circuit of this device is used as a bistable multivibrator with the circuit activated by switch S1. Output level remains at zero, set by the voltage applied to the threshold input pin 2 until one of the alarm contact switches is closed, causing C1 to discharge.

"Press-for off" alarm switches can be fitted to the doors, bonnet and boot lid, so arranged that opening a door or lid completes that switch contact. This produces an output signal for about 8 seconds, pulling in the relay after an initial delay of about 4 seconds. The horn circuit is completed by the relay contacts, so the horn will sound for 8 seconds. After this, the relay drops out (shutting off the horn) until capacitor C1 charges up again. This takes about 3 seconds, when the relay pulls in once more and the horn sounds again. This varying signal of 8 seconds horn on, 3 seconds horn off, is repeated until switch S1 is turned off (or the battery is dead). This type of alarm signal commands more attention than a continuous sounding alarm.

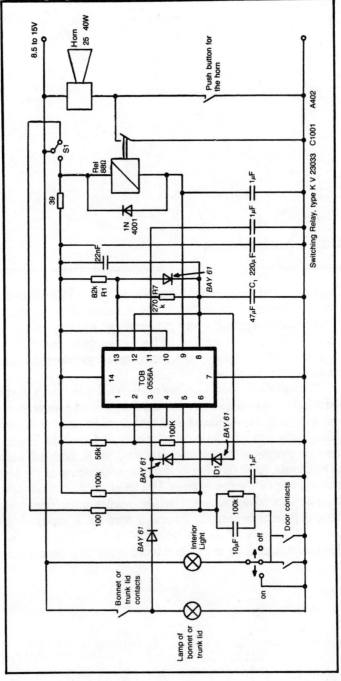

Fig. 2-1. Circuit design for a car theft alarm.

4

PROJECT 3:
Electric Motor Speed Controller

A variety of ICs are designed as speed regulators for small dc motors such as those used in portable cassette players, movie cameras, models, and toys. The object is to govern the motor so that it runs at a constant speed, independent of variations in battery supply voltage and load on the motor. The TDA1151 is selected for the following circuits, having a maximum rating of 20 volts (which covers most model and other small dc motors), with an output current of up to 800 milliamps. It is a flat rectangular plastic package with three leads emerging from one end, and it comprises 18 transistors, 4 diodes and 7 resistors in a linear integrated circuit.

In its simplest application, it is used with a potentiometer (R_s) acting as a speed regulation resistance (and by which the actual motor speed is adjusted); and a torque control resistor (R_t) which provides automatic regulation against load on the motor. Both of these resistors are bridged by capacitors, although C2 can be omitted (see Fig. 3-1). Component values shown in Table 3-1 are suitable for a 6- to 12-volt supply.

A slightly different circuit is shown in Fig. 3-2, using a TCA600/900 or TCA610/910 integrated circuit. These have maximum voltage ratings of 14 and 20 volts respectively and maximum current ratings of 400 milliamps for starting, but only 140 milliamps for continuous running.

Devices of this type work on the principle of providing a constant output voltage to the motor independent of variations in sup-

5

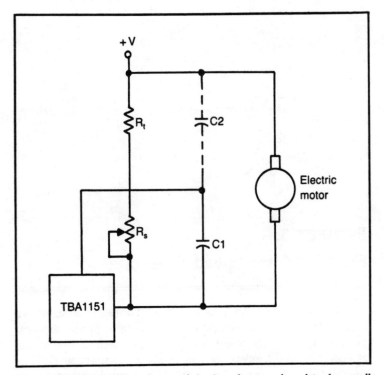

Fig. 3-1. The TDA1151 linear integrated circuit used as a speed regulator for a small dc electric motor.

ply voltage, the value of this voltage being set by adjustment of R_s. At the same time, the device can generate a negative output resistance to compensate speed fluctuations due to variations in torque. This negative output resistance is equal to RT/K, where K is a constant, depending on the parameters of the device, as demonstrated in Table 3-2.

The table also shows the reference voltage (V_{ref}) and quiescent current drain (I_o) of the three ICs mentioned.

Table 3-1.

R_s	1 KΩ
R_t	280 Ω
C1	10 μF to 2 μF
C2(if used)	25 μF

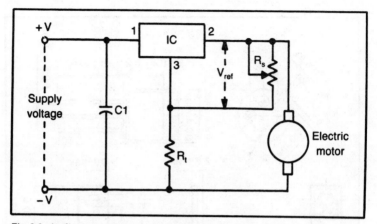

Fig. 3-2. Application circuit for the TCA600/610 or TCA900/910 motor speed regulators. R_s is the speed regulation resistor (variable). R_t is the torque control resistor. A suitable value for C1 is 0.1F. A diode can be added in line 3 to provide temperature compensation as well.

The following relationships then apply for calculating suitable component values for these circuits:

$$R_t = K \bullet R_M$$

where R_M is the typical motor resistance.

$$\text{Minimum value of Rs} = \frac{V_{ref} \bullet RT}{Eg - (V_{ref} - 1_o RT)}$$

where Eg = back *emf* of motor at required or rated speed, and I_o = quiescent current drain of the device. Actual voltage developed across the motor given by:

$$\text{Volts (at motor)} = R_M \bullet I_M + Eg$$

where I_m is the current drain by the motor at the required or rated speed.

The physical appearance of these chips can be seen in Fig. 3-3, while Fig. 3-4 shows the complex internal circuitry within one of these chips.

Table 3-2.

IC	K(typical)	V_{ref}	I_o	
TDA1151	20	1.2	1.7	mA
TCA600/900	8.5	2.6	2.6	mA
TCA610/910	8.5	2.6	2.6	mA

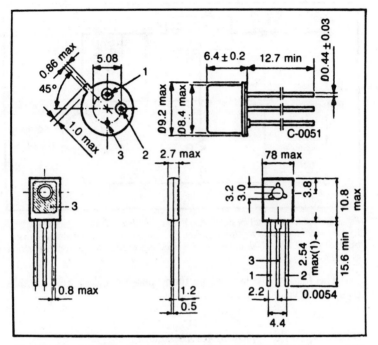

Fig. 3-3. Physical appearance of the TCA600/610 in a TO-39 metal can and the TCA900/910 in a flat plastic package.

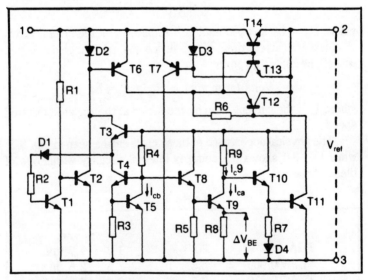

Fig. 3-4. Although small devices, these integrated circuits for motor speed control are based on the complicated circuitry shown here.

PROJECT 4:
Digital Clock

Counter circuits can be used to build digital clocks and timers (clock in the usual sense—a device that tells you what time of day it is). The first thing you need when designing an electronic timepiece is an accurate timebase. This is basically the same as the clock oscillators used to keep various digital circuits in synchronization. A digital time-telling clock essentially counts the numbers of seconds, minutes, and hours. Of course, it needs some way to know just how long a second is so it can be counted. The timebase generates a signal with a precise frequency so that the circuitry can count x number of pulses per second.

This timebase frequency must be extremely accurate. It might seem like there is little difference between .95 second and 1 second, but when you multiply that 5% error over a 24-hour day, you end up with a 22-hour, 48-minute day. That's not very good timekeeping. About the only thing that kind of clock would be useful for is paperweight duty!

Most electronic clock circuits work with a timebase of 60 Hz (60 pulses per second). This tradition stems from the ac electric power lines that operate at a 60 Hz rate. An electrically powered clock can use the ac power source itself as a timebase. Adapting the ac power signal for use in a digital circuit is difficult, and with modern technology, it's more trouble than it's worth.

Most digital clocks work with some sort of crystal oscillator. Quartz crystals make very precisely held frequencies possible.

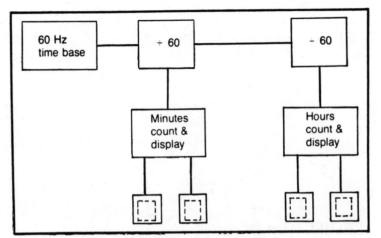

Fig. 4-1. The complete clock project is shown here in block diagram form.

Incidentally, when digital watches first became popular, many were proudly touted in the ads as being quartz-controlled. *All* digital watches are quartz-controlled. A crystal oscillator is used for the timebase, and crystals are slices of quartz. See Fig. 4-1 for a block diagram of this circuit.

Most crystals operate at frequencies much higher than 60 Hz. Generally, their resonant frequencies are above 1 MHz (1,000,000 Hz). Additional counter stages are needed to drop this frequency down. The MM5369 (shown in Fig. 4-2) is a specially designed IC for just this purpose. It generates an extremely precise and stable 60 Hz timebase signal from a 3.579545 (generally shortened to 3.58) MHz (3,579,545 Hz) crystal. This particular input frequency was selected because it is the frequency used in colorburst oscillators in color TV sets, so they are readily available.

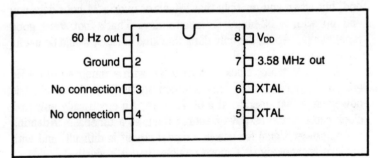

Fig. 4-2. The MM5369 is an 8-pin IC that can generate a precise and reliable 60 Hz timebase signal.

10

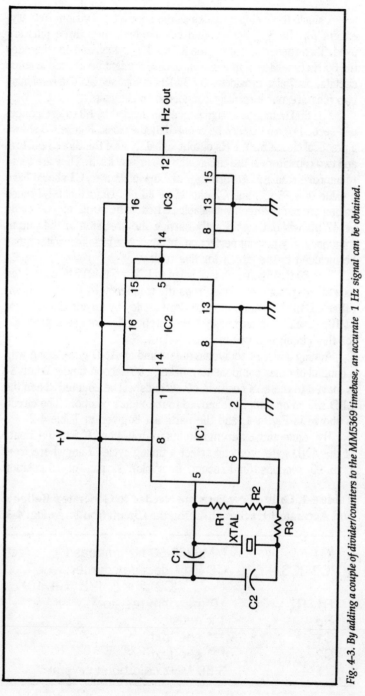

Fig. 4-3. By adding a couple of divider/counters to the MM5369 timebase, an accurate 1 Hz signal can be obtained.

A single 8-pin chip provides all the necessary division. Actually, except for the V_{DD} and ground connections, only three pins are used. Two connections go to the 3.58 MHz crystal, and one provides the 60 Hz timebase output signal. In case it might be needed in some circuits, pin 7 also provides a 3.58 MHz output signal. The remaining two pins are not internally connected to the chip.

The 60 Hz timebase signal must be divided by 60 to get a once-per-second signal that can be counted by the clock. Figure 4-3 shows a practical circuit for a 1 Hz output signal. Notice the three resistors and two capacitors in the circuit with the crystal itself. They are there to improve stability. According to the manufacturer, C1 should have a value of 6.36 pF, and C2 should be 30 pF. Unfortunately, these values are not commonly available. C1 could be 10 pF and C2 could be 47 pF without significantly hurting the precision of the output frequency. If you want perfection, trimmer (variable) capacitors may be included in the circuit for fine tuning.

The 60 Hz timebase signal is fed to IC2, a CD4017 IC connected as a six-step counter. This drops the frequency to 10Hz. IC3, another CD4017, divides the signal frequency by an additional factor of 10, resulting in a precise 1 Hz output. The complete parts list for this circuit is given in Table 4-1.

Adding a pair of additional timers and an AND gate, along with a handful of other components, makes a 60-second timer. When S1 is moved to the RUN position, 60 seconds will be counted. Then the LED will go on until S1 is moved to the RESET position. The circuit is shown in Fig. 4-4, and the parts list is given in Table 4-2.

By connecting different outputs from IC4 and IC5 to the inputs of the AND gate, you can select a timing cycle of anywhere from 1 to 99 seconds (in 1-second intervals). A pair of 10-position

Table 4-1. Only a Few Parts are Needed to Generate a Reliable and Accurate 1 Hz Signal, Using the Circuit Shown in Fig. 4-3.

IC1	MM5369 60 Hz timebase
IC2, IC3	CD4017 decade counter
	(IC2 = ÷ 6, IC3 = ÷ 10)
R1, R2	10 megohm resistor
R3	1 k resistor
C1	*** see text
C2	*** see text
XTAL	3.58 MHz colorburst crystal

Table 4-2. Parts List for the 60-Second Timer Circuit of Fig. 4-4.

IC1 - IC3	see Table 4-1
R1 - R3	see Table 4-1
C1, C2	see Table 4-1
XTAL	see Table 4-1
IC4, IC5	CD4017 decade counter
IC6	CD4081 quad AND gate
D1	LED
R4	330 ohm resistor
S1	SPDT switch

thumbwheel switches can turn this project into a fine programmable timer.

Another useful modification to this project is shown in Fig. 4-5 (parts list in Table 4-3). By replacing the AND gate (IC6 in Fig. 4-4) with this circuit (using a single quad NAND gate package and a handful of discrete components), when the timing period is over, the LED lights and a tone sounds until the circuit is reset. IC6A and IC6B behave like the original AND gate, while IC6C and IC6D are connected as a tone generator with an output of approximately 1 kHz (1000 Hz).

Back-tracking somewhat, connecting the 1 Hz source circuit of Fig. 4-3 to the input of the circuit illustrated in Fig. 4-6, will provide a clock with minute readouts from 00 to 59. Once the count reaches 60, the counters are reset to 00. The count is displayed on a pair

Table 4-3. These Components can be Added to the 60-Second Timer Circuit of Fig. 4-4 to Add an Audible Alarm. The Circuitry is Shown in Fig. 4-5.

Eliminate IC6, R4, and D1 in Fig. 4-3 and replace with:	
IC6	CD4011 quad NAND gate
D1	LED
R4	330 ohm resistor
R5	1 megohm resistor
R6	100 k resistor
R7	100 ohm resistor
C3	0.01 μF disc capacitor

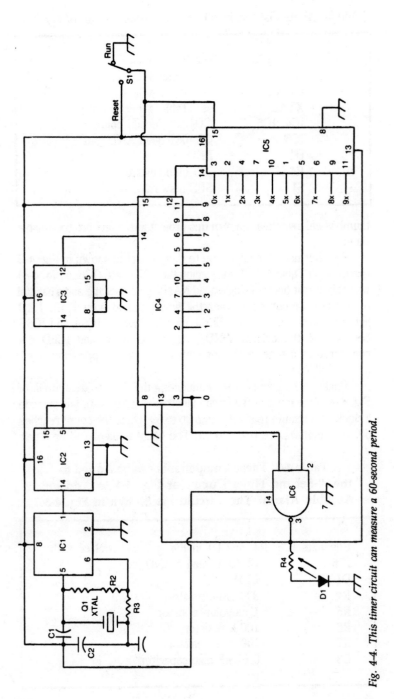

Fig. 4-4. This timer circuit can measure a 60-second period.

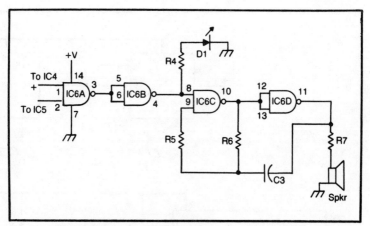

Fig. 4-5. Adding these components to the 60-second timer circuit of Fig. 4-4 will cause a tone to be sounded when the circuit times out.

**Table 4-4. The Minutes Portion
of a Practical Digital Clock can be Constructed
Using These Components Wired as Shown in Fig. 4-6.**

IC4,IC5	CD4017 decade counter
IC6	CD4518 dual BCD counter
IC7	CD4011 quad NAND gate
IC8,IC9	CD4511 BCD-to-7-segment decoder
DIS1, DIS2	Seven-segment LED display, common cathode
R4,R7	330 ohm resistor

**Table 4-5. List of Parts for
the Hours Display Circuitry Illustrated in Fig. 4-6.**

IC10,IC11	CD4017 decade counter
IC12	CD4518 dual BCD counter
IC13	CD4511 BCD-to-7-segment decoder
IC14	CD4011 quad NAND gate
IC15	CD4049 hex inverter
DIS3, DIS4	Seven-segment LED display, common cathode
R18-R30	330 ohm resistor

15

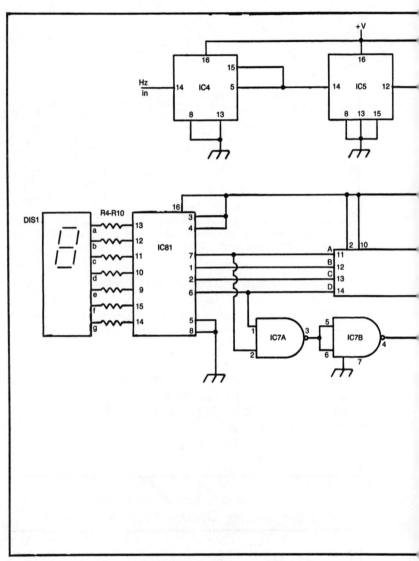

Fig. 4-6. This circuit can display the minutes counter in a digital clock.

of seven-segment LED displays. The parts list for this subcircuit
is given in Table 4-4.

Figure 4-7 shows the circuitry for adding the display for hours
(ranging from 01 to 12). IC10 and IC11 count each group of 60
minutes. Alternatively, the signal from the minutes counter reset
(from IC7C and D) could be used to trigger the hours counter.

16

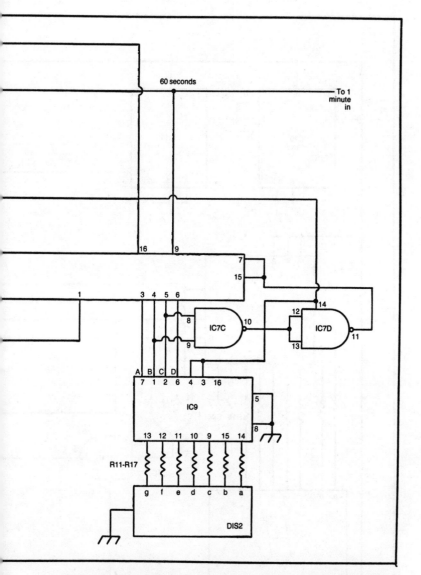

The ones digit is wired in the usual fashion, but the tens column can use a few shortcuts. This digit will always be either 0 or 1. Segments b and c will always be lit, so they are tied directly to the positive power supply (through current dropping resistors). If the count is less than 10, then segments a, d, e, and f are lit to produce a 0. Segment g is never lit. The parts list for the hours display circuit is given in Table 4-5.

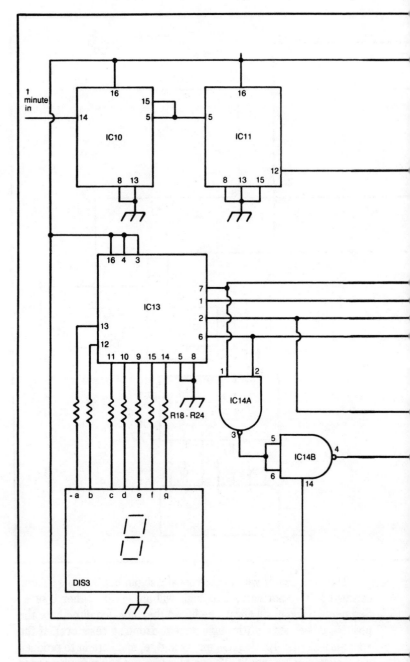

Fig. 4-7. The hours portion of a digital clock is controlled using this circuit.

18

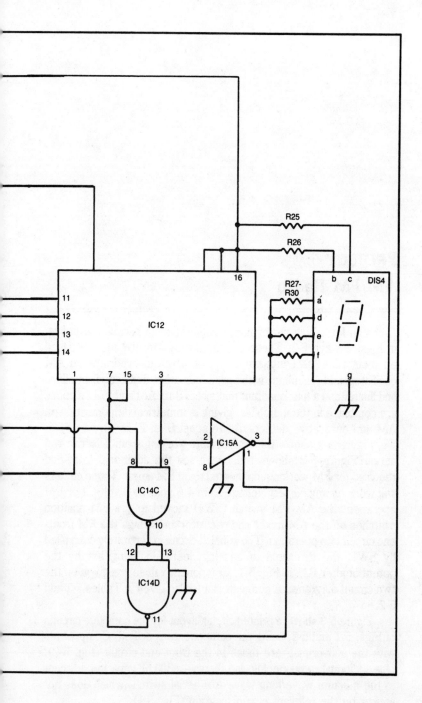

19

PROJECT 5:
AM/FM Radio

A design for a high performance AM/FM radio receiver is shown in Figs. 5-1 and 5-2. These circuits are by Mullard and are based on their TDA 1071 integrated circuit which incorporates an AM oscillator, and AM mixer with agc, a four-stage differential amplifier and limiter and a four-quadrant multiplier. Both AM and FM functions are combined in the multiplier, giving symmetrical demodulation on AM and quadrative detection with squelch on FM.

Figure 5-1 shows the AM circuit, working from a ferrite rod aerial. Figure 5-2 shows the circuit for the additional front-end required for FM working, connected to an FM aerial. These circuits will work on any battery voltage from 4.5 volts to 9 volts. For FM operation, the AM-FM switch (SW4) moved to the FM position switches off the AM mixer and oscillator and brings the FM front-end circuit into operation. The squelch circuit is separately controlled by SW1, the threshold of squelch operation being set by the potentiometer R11 in Fig. 5-1. Component values are given on the two circuit diagrams. A complete list is also given in Tables 5-1 and 5-2.

Figure 5-3 shows a printed circuit layout for the complete circuits of Figs. 5-1 and 5-2, using the components specified. Components with the subscript F are those in the front-end circuit (Fig. 5-2). One additional component is also shown—a 300 pF capacitor adjacent to the medium wave/long wave AM aerial switch, which does not appear on the relevant circuit diagram (Fig. 5-1).

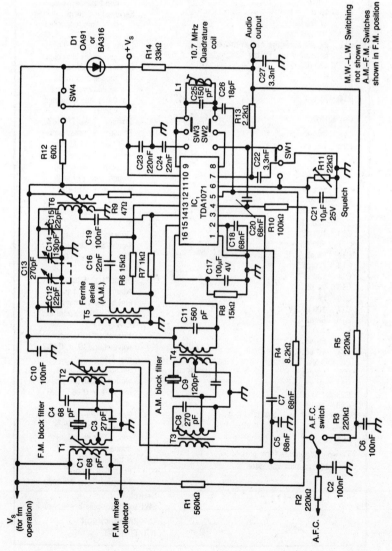

Fig. 5-1. Circuit diagram of AM/FM receiver using the TDA1071 integrated circuit (Mullard).

21

Table 5-1. Parts for the AM/FM Receiver Circuit.

Resistors

All resistors CR25 10% unless stated

R1	500 KΩ
R2	220 KΩ
R3	220 KΩ
R4	8.2 KΩ
R5	220 KΩ
R6	15 KΩ
R7	1 KΩ
R8	15 Ω
R9	47 Ω
R10	100 KΩ
R11	22 KΩ Miniature carbon preset potentiometer, Philips 2322 410 03309
R12	68 Ω
R13	2.2 KΩ
R14	33 KΩ

Capacitors

C1	68 pF
C2	100 nF
C3	27 pF
C4	68 pF
N5	68 nF
C6	100 nF
C7	68 nF
C8	270 pF
C9	120 pF
C10	100 nF
C11	560 pF
C12	22 pF
C13	270 pF*
C14	130 pF*
C15	22 pF
C16	22 nF
C17	100 μF,4V
C18	68 nF
C19	100 nF
C20	68 nF
C21	10 μF, 25V
C22	3.3 nF
C23	230 nF
C24	22 nF
C25	150 pF
C26	18 pF
C27	3.3 pF

*These components form part of the ganged tuning capacitor

Winding data

T1	Primary: 12 turns, 0.071 mm enameled copper Secondary: 2 turns, tapped at 1 turn, 0.071 mm enameled copper Former: Toko 7P 0092
T2	Primary: 12 turns, tapped at 1 turn, 0.071 mm enameled copper Secondary: 3 turns, 0.071 mm enameled copper
T3	Primary: 3 turns, 0.071 mm enameled copper Secondary: 120 turns, tapped at 5 turns, wound over primary, 0.071 mm enameled copper Former: Toko 7P0089
T4	Primary: 9 turns, tapped at 5 turns, 0.071 mm enameled copper Secondary: 86 turns, wound over primary, 0.071 mm enameled copper Former: Toko 0089
T5	M.W— Primary: 78 turns, wound in a single layer, 3 × 3 × 3 × 0.063 mm litz Secondary: 4 turns wound over the earthy end of the primary 3 × 3 × 3 × 0.063 mm litz L.W.— Primary: 210 turns, wavewound, 9 × 0.063 mm litz Secondary: 12 turns, wound under the primary, 9 × 0.063 mm litz For T5, the coils are mounted on a ferrite rod, 178 mm in length, diameter 9.5 mm.
L1	8 turns, 0.071 mm enameled copper. Former: Toko 7P 0092

Switch
SW1 to SW4 4-pole 2-way switch

Integrated circuit
IC1 TDA1071

Table 5-2. Parts for the FM Front End Circuit.

Resistors		Capacitors	
All resistors CR25 10%		C1	18 pF
R1	1.2 KΩ	C2	3.3 nF
R2	12 KΩ	C3	4.7 pF
R3	27 KΩ	C4	3.3 nF
R4	27 KΩ	C5	12 pF*
R5	12 KΩ	C6	18 pF
R6	1 KΩ	C7	3.3 nF
R7	39 Ω	C8	18 pF
R8	27 KΩ	C9	12 pF*
R9	12 KΩ	C10	3.3 nF
R10	100 Ω	C11	2.7 pF
R11	10 Ω	C12	5.6 pF
R12	1 KΩ	C13	3.3 nF
R13	39 Ω	C14	56 pF
		C15	3.3 nF
		C16	22 nF

Transistors		Diode	
TR1, TR2, TR3	BF195	D1	BB110

Winding data

T1	Primary: 2 turns, 0.031 mm enameled copper
	Secondary: 2 turns, 0.031 mm enameled copper
	Former: Neosid 5 mm with ferrite core
T2	Primary: 4 turns, spaced one diameter 0.71 mm enameled copper
	Secondary: 1 turn, interwound with the primary 0.71 mm enameled copper
	Former: Neosid 5 mm with ferrite core
L1	3 turns, spaced one diameter and tapped at 1 1/2 turns, 0.71 mm enameled copper
	Former: Neosid 5 mm with ferrite core

*These components form part of the ganged turning capacitor

Note also that this circuit is complete only up to the audio output stage—i.e., it needs to be followed by an audio amplifier and speaker(s)—see Projects 6 and 7 for possible circuits to use.

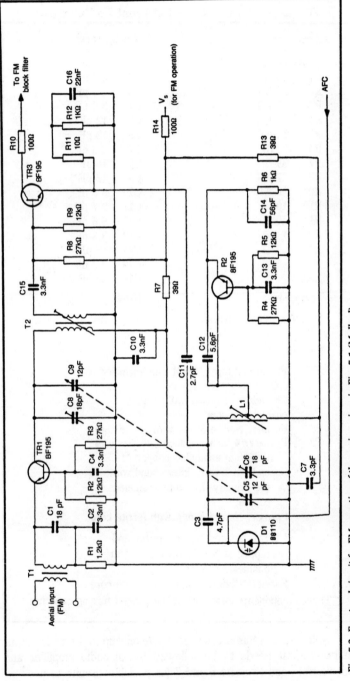

Fig. 5-2. Front-end circuit for FM operation of the receiver given in Fig. 5-1 (Mullard).

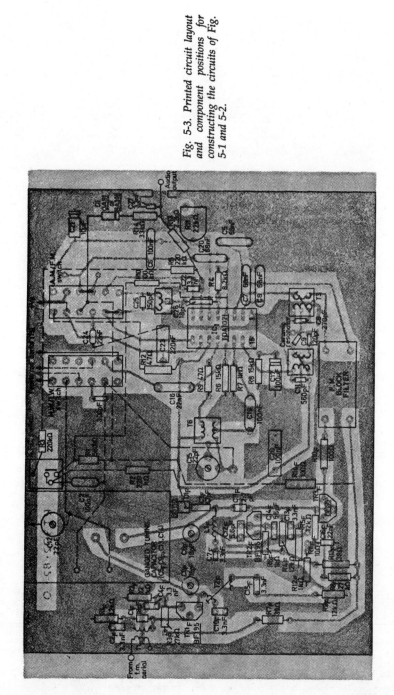

Fig. 5-3. Printed circuit layout and component positions for constructing the circuits of Fig. 5-1 and 5-2.

PROJECT 6:
Audio Amplifiers

Quite a number of linear ICs are designed as audio amplifiers for use in radio receivers, record players, etc. Again these are used with external components, but physical layout and the length of leads is relatively unimportant—unlike circuits carrying radio frequencies. The "packaging" of such ICs can vary from cans to dual-in-line and quad-in-line. They usually have 12 or 14 leads (sometimes less). Not all these leads are necessarily used in a working circuit. They are there to provide access to different parts of the integrated circuit for different applications. Integrated circuits designed with higher power ratings sometimes incorporate a tab (or tabs) or a copper slug on top of the package to be connected to a heatsink.

A single chip can contain one, two, three or more amplifier stages interconnected and following each other (technically referred to as being in *cascade*). Pinout connections provide "tapping" points for using one or more stages separately or in cascade as required.

The (RCA) CA3035 integrated circuit is just one example. It consists of three separate amplifier stages connected in cascade with a component count equivalent to 10 transistors, 1 diode, and 15 resistors. Each amplifier stage has different characteristics. The first stage, which can be selected by connections to pins 1, 2, 3, 9, and 10 (see Fig. 6-1), is a wide band amplifier characterized by high input resistance (i.e., ideally suited to connecting to a preceding transistor

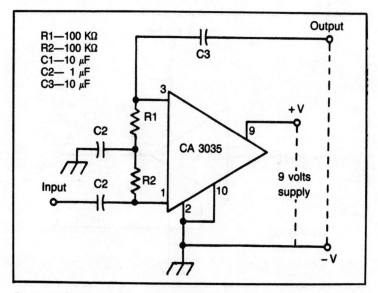

Fig. 6-1. *Utilization of the first amplifier in CA3035 integrated circuit by tapping pins 1, 2, 3, 9 and 10. This circuit gives a voltage gain of 100-160 with an input resistance of 50 KΩ and an output resistance of 270 Ω.*

stage). The working circuit using this stage is in Fig. 6-1. It has a gain of the order of 160 (44 dB).

The second amplifier in the CA3035 has a lower input resistance (2 KΩ) and a low output resistance of 170 Ω. The gain is similar to

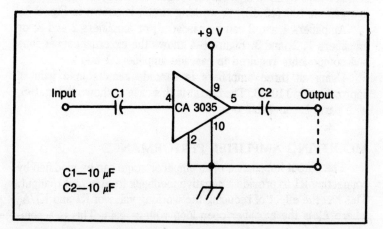

Fig. 6-2. *Utilization of the second amplifier in CA3035 integrated circuit by tapping pins 2, 4, 5, 9 and 10. This circuit gives a voltage gain of 100-120 with an input resistance of 2 Ω and an output resistance of 170 Ω.*

27

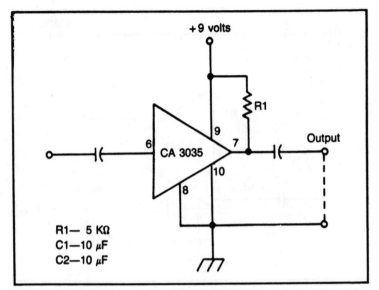

Fig. 6-3. Utilization of the third amplifier in CA3035 integrated circuit by tapping pins 6, 7, 8, 9 and 10. This circuit gives a voltage gain of 80-120 with an input resistance of 670 Ω and an output resistance of 5 KΩ.

the first stage (about 45 dB). A working circuit with tapping points is shown in Fig. 6-2.

The third amplifier is a wide band amplifier with a low input resistance (670 Ω) and a high output resistance (5 KΩ). It offers a voltage gain of 100 (40 dB). A working circuit is shown in Fig. 6-3.

Amplifiers 1 and 2 can be cascaded; or amplifiers 2 and 3; or amplifiers 1, 2, and 3. Figure 6-4 shows the external connections and components required to cascade amplifiers 1 and 2.

Using all three amplifiers in cascade results in a gain of approximately 110 dB. The circuit in this case is shown in Fig. 6-5, with parts list in Table 6-1.

MODIFYING AMPLIFIER PERFORMANCE

The output impedance of an amplifier stage can be modified by connecting R1 to provide a negative feedback from output to input. This has the effect of reducing the working value of R1 and $R1/A_v$ where A_v is the amplifier open loop voltage gain. This is accomplished without affecting the actual voltage gain. In the case of cascaded amplifiers, a capacitor C2 is needed in series with R1 to block dc (i.e., R1 only is needed for amplifier 1 because C1 is effective

28

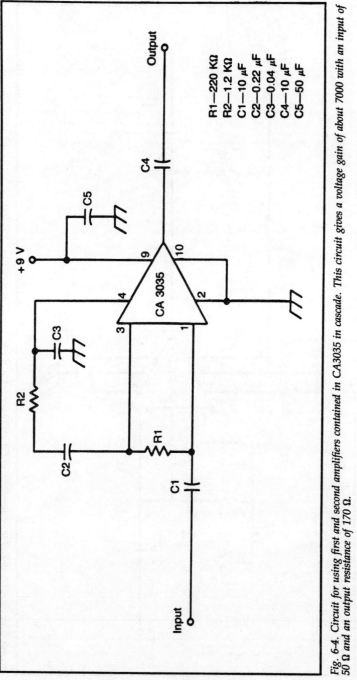

R1—220 KΩ
R2—1.2 KΩ
C1—10 μF
C2—0.22 μF
C3—0.04 μF
C4—10 μF
C5—50 μF

Fig. 6-4. Circuit for using first and second amplifiers contained in CA3035 in cascade. This circuit gives a voltage gain of about 7000 with an input of 50 Ω and an output resistance of 170 Ω.

29

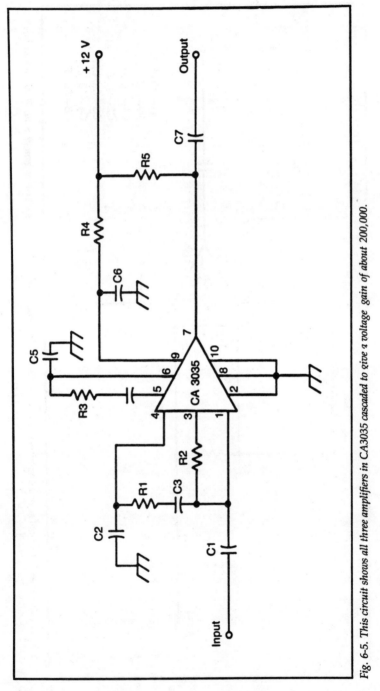

Fig. 6-5. This circuit shows all three amplifiers in CA3035 cascaded to give a voltage gain of about 200,000.

30

Table 6-1. Parts List for Fig. 6-5.

R1	220 KΩ	C1	10 μF
R2	1.2 KΩ	C2	0.04 μF
R3	680Ω	C3	0.22 μF
R4	1 KΩ	C4	0.05 μF
R5	4.7 KΩ	C5	0.05 μF
		C6	50 μF
		C7	10 μF

as a blocking capacitor in this case). Because amplifier 2 in this chip is directly coupled to amplifier 1 and amplifier 2 is directly coupled to amplifier 3, the use of an impedance-matching resistor applied to amplifier 2 (or amplifier 3) requires the use of a blocking capacitor in series with the resistor.

The gain of the amplifier stage can be modified by the use of a series resistor in the input (R1). This acts as a potential divider in conjunction with the effective input resistance of the stage so that only a proportion of the input signal is applied to the stage. In this case:

$$\text{Actual Voltage Gain} = \frac{R1}{R_i + R1/A_v}$$

$$\text{Input Resistance} = R_i + R1/A_v$$

where R_i is the input resistance of the IC.

Thus, by suitable choice of R1 and R_i, both voltage gain and input resistance of an amplifier circuit can be modified to match specific requirements. It follows that if a number of different resistors are used for R_i, the circuit can be given different response (sensitivity) for a given input applied to each value of R_i by switching. This mode of working is useful for preamplifiers. Virtually the same circuit is used for an audio mixer, separate input channels being connected by separate series resistors (R_i) and commonly connected to the input. In this case, each channel has the same input resistance with an overall gain of unity.

PROJECT 7:
Power Amplifiers

Because amplifiers are used in one form or another in almost every electronic system, it is not surprising that a great many amplifier ICs have been developed for various applications. Some have incredibly impressive specifications. It is often surprising to see how much power can be packed into the tiny IC chip.

For the most efficient and reliable performance, IC amplifiers should always be used with adequate heatsinking. In many cases, the better the heatsinking, the greater the maximum output power can be. When in doubt about how much heatsinking to use, try to err on the side of too much rather than too little. The chief disadvantage of using a heatsink that is too large is that the device would take up a little more space. The disadvantages of using an insufficient heatsink include inferior performance and possibly thermal damage to expensive components.

It would be futile to attempt to compile a complete list of available amplifier ICs. Hundreds of devices are already on the market, with more appearing every month. A so-called "complete" listing would be out of date before it came off the presses.

This chapter looks at a few representative examples of amplifier ICs of various types. The only kind of amplifier IC that will not be discussed in this chapter is the op amp.

Emphasis in this chapter is on audio amplifier ICs, because these are the most widely available and of the most interest to experimenters.

THE LM380 AUDIO AMPLIFIER IC

The LM380 is an audio amplifier IC that has been around for quite a few years now and still enjoys considerable popularity. Judging from the industrial and hobbyist literature, this chip appears to be the most popular amplifier device around.

The LM380 is widely available, and it comes in two packaging styles, an 8-pin DIP and a 14-pin DIP. The pinout for the 8-pin version is shown in Fig. 7-1, while the 14-pin version is illustrated in Fig. 7-2. Notice that the 14-pin version does not have any additional pin functions. On both packages, only six of the pins are actually active. The remaining pins are shorted to ground and provide some internal heatsinking. Since the 14-pin LM380 has more heatsink pins than the 8-pin version, it can handle greater amounts of power without overheating. There are no other differences between the two package types.

Without any external heatsinking, the basic LM380 can dissipate up to about 1.25 watts at room temperature. This certainly isn't bad for an amplifier less than the size of your thumbnail, but the LM380 can put out even more power with external heatsinking. For instance, if a 14-pin LM380 is mounted on a PC board with 2-ounce foil, and the six heatsink pins are soldered to a 6-square-inch copper foil pad, the IC can produce up to about 3.7 watts at room temperature. This is an impressive, almost threefold increase in power at very little additional cost.

This chip also features an internal automatic thermal shutdown circuit that turns the amplifier off if excessive current flow causes

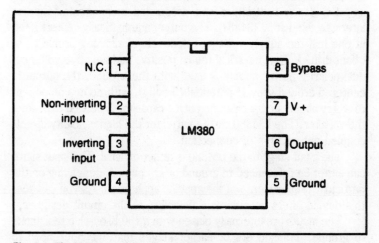

Fig. 7-1. The LM380 amplifier IC, available in an 8-pin DIP housing.

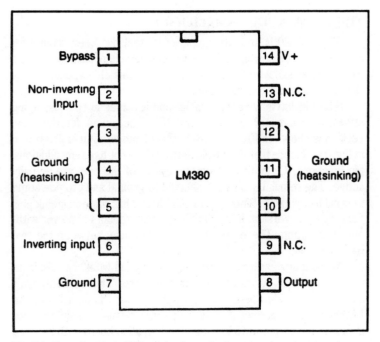

Fig. 7-2. Even the 14-pin DIP version has only six active pins; the extra pins are used for heatsinking.

the IC to start overheating. This feature significantly reduces the worry of short-circuit problems.

As illustrated in Fig. 7-3, the LM380's internal circuitry is made up of a dozen transistors and associated components. Gain is internally fixed at 50 (34 dB). The output automatically centers itself at one half the supply voltage, effectively eliminating problems of offset drift. If a symmetrical (equal positive and negative voltages) dual-polarity power supply is used with the LM380, the output is centered around ground potential (0 volts), with no dc component to worry about. In this case, no output capacitor is needed to protect the speaker. The LM380 can be wired for the higher fidelity direct-coupled output type of connection.

The input stage of the LM380 is rather unusual. The input signal can either be referenced to ground or ac coupled, depending on the particular requirements of the specific application. As you can see, this device offers considerable flexibility to the circuit designer.

The inputs are internally biased with a 150 K on-chip resistance to ground. Transducers or earlier stages that are referenced to

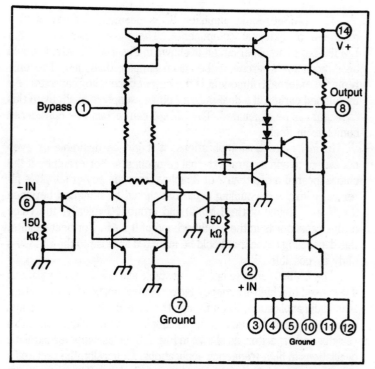

Fig. 7-3. A simplified diagram of the internal circuitry in the LM380 amplifier IC.

ground (no dc component) can be directly coupled to either the inverting or the non-inverting input. (These inputs are similar to those found on op amps. The inverting input phase shifts the signal 180 degrees, while the non-inverting input does not phase shift the signal).

In most applications, only one of the LM380's inputs is used. There are several possibilities for handling the unused input terminal:

- Leave it floating
- Short it directly to ground
- Reference it to ground through an external resistor or capacitor

In many applications in which the non-inverting input is used, the inverting input is left floating (unconnected). This is fine, but it makes board layout critical. The designer must be on guard for any stray capacitances. While it is always true that stray capacitances can lead to positive feedback, instability, and possible oscillations, this configuration is particularly susceptible to such problems.

The LM380 audio amplifier IC is designed for use with a minimum of external components. The most basic form of a LM380-based amplifier circuit is shown in Fig. 7-4. Clearly, it would be difficult for a circuit to be much simpler than this. The only required external component is the output decoupling capacitor. As mentioned earlier, if a dual-polarity power supply is used, even this capacitor can be eliminated. The LM380 can certainly be considered complete in itself.

In many practical applications, it might be desirable or even necessary to add several external components. For example, if the chip is located more than 2 or 3 inches from the power supply's filter capacitor, a decoupling capacitor should be mounted between the V + terminal of the LM380 and ground. Typically, the value of this capacitor is in the neighborhood of 0.1 μF. For best results, this decoupling capacitor should be mounted as close to the LM380's body as possible.

The LM380 tends to become unstable and break into oscillations if it is used in a high-frequency (several megahertz or more) rather than audio application. Even though this IC is designated as an audio amplifier, it can function as an rf amplifier too. Adding an extra resistor and capacitor, as shown in Fig. 7-5, helps suppress parasitic oscillations in high-frequency applications. Generally, the resistor's value is very small. A typical value is 2.7 ohms. The capacitor is usually about 0.1 μF.

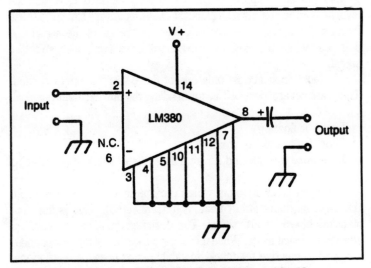

Fig. 7-4. The most basic circuit built around the LM380 amplifier IC.

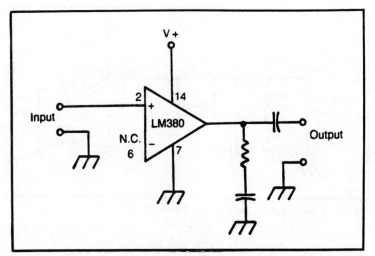

Fig. 7-5. Adding a resistor and a capacitor to the circuit of Fig. 7-4 helps minimize oscillation problems.

Because these parasitic oscillations only occur at 5 to 10 MHz, they obviously won't be of much importance in most audio applications. Even so, if the LM380 is being used in an rf-sensitive environment, such oscillations could pose a problem unless they are properly suppressed.

(Note that in Fig. 7-5 and all the future diagrams that the heat-sinking pins are not shown. This is for clarity in the circuit diagrams. The grounding of these pins is assumed in all cases.)

Figure 7-6 shows a practical audio amplifier circuit using the LM380. A typical parts list for this project is given in Table 7-1.

The input to this circuit can be provided by an inexpensive low impedance microphone, like those sold for use with portable cassette recorders. If a low impedance source is used, an impedance matching transformer is necessary. If this circuit is to be used with a high-impedance source, this transformer can be eliminated.

The 1 MΩ potentiometer serves as a volume control. The fixed gain of this circuit can be increased by adding a little positive feedback.

An 8 Ω speaker can be driven directly by the LM380 audio amplifier IC. The output decoupling capacitor is needed if a single-polarity power supply is used, as shown in the diagram.

The LM380 is often used in inexpensive tape recorders and phonographs. Figure 7-7 shows a simple phonograph amplifier circuit. The input in this case is a ceramic cartridge. The parts list is given

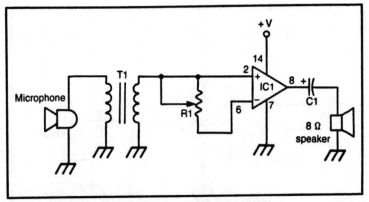

Fig. 7-6. A practical audio amplifier circuit using the LM380.

Table 7-1. Parts List for Fig. 7-6.

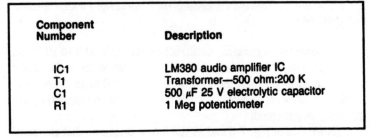

Component Number	Description
IC1	LM380 audio amplifier IC
T1	Transformer—500 ohm:200 K
C1	500 μF 25 V electrolytic capacitor
R1	1 Meg potentiometer

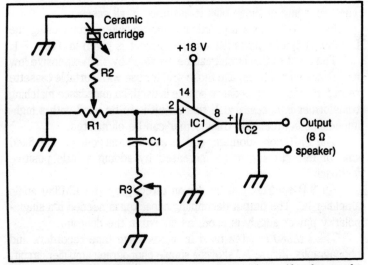

Fig. 7-7. The LM380 is ideal for use in inexpensive ceramic cartridge phonographs.

Table 7-2. Parts List for Fig. 7-7.

Component Number	Description
IC1	LM380 audio amplifier IC
C1	0.047 µF capacitor
C2	500 µF electrolytic capacitor
R1	25 K potentiometer
R2	75 K resistor
R3	10 K potentiometer

in Table 7-2. Potentiometer R1 is a simple voltage-divider volume control. Potentiometer R3 is a basic tone control, making the high frequency roll-off characteristics of the circuit manually adjustable.

Most serious phonograph applications require frequency shaping to provide the standard RIAA equalization characteristic. All commercially available records are equalized according to the RIAA standards. Obviously, if the complementary frequency-response shaping isn't included in the playback, the reproduced sound won't be as good as it should be.

Figure 7-8 shows a LM380-based phonograph amplifier circuit with full RIAA equalization. The parts list is given in Table 7-3.

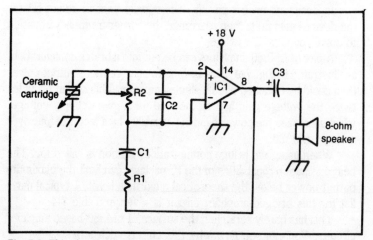

Fig. 7-8. This phonograph amplifier includes RIAA equalization.

Table 7-3. Parts List for Fig. 7-8.

Component Number	Description
IC1	LM380 audio amplifier IC
C1	220 pF capacitor
C2	0.0022 μF capacitor
C3	500 μF electrolytic capacitor
R1	1.5 Meg resistor
R2	2 Meg potentiometer

The mid-band gain can be defined with this formula:

$$G = (R1 + 150000) / 150000$$

The constant 150000 represents the internal resistance presented within the LM380 itself. R1 is the value of the external resistor.

The corner frequency is determined by resistor R1 and capacitor C1, according to this formula:

$$F_c = \frac{1}{2\pi C_1 R_1}$$

In designing such a circuit, it is usually best to select R1 for the desired gain first, then rearrange the corner frequency equation to solve for C1.

A pair of LM380 amplifiers can be put into a bridge configuration, as illustrated in Fig. 7-9. This is done to achieve more output power than could be obtained from a single amplifier. This circuit provides twice the voltage gain across the load for a given supply voltage, which increases the power handling capability by a factor of four over a single LM380.

When using the bridge configuration, caution is called for. The heat dissipation capabilities of the IC package can limit the maximum output power below the theoretical quadruple level. A typical parts list for this bridged-amplifier circuit is given in Table 7-4.

This has barely scratched the surface of LM380-based amplifier circuits. You can see now why this chip is such a best-seller.

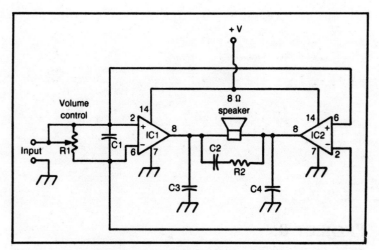

Fig. 7-9. A pair of LM380s in a bridge configuration can produce greater output power.

Table 7-4. Parts List for Fig. 7-9.

Component Number	Description
IC1, IC2	LM380 audio amplifier IC
C1	50 pF capacitor
C2, C3, C4	0.1 μF capacitor
R1	2 Meg potentiometer
R2	2 Ω resistor

PROJECT 8:
Tape Player Amplifier

The circuit shown in Fig. 8-1 is designed as a playback amplifier for a tape deck. The standard NAB equalization curve is matched by the feedback network. The parts list is shown in Table 8-1.

The tape head should be selected to generate about 800 μV at 1 kHz. The output is approximately 5 volts rms. An external volume control potentiometer can be added to the output line.

Table 8-1.

IC	CA 381
R1	240 KΩ
R2	180 Ω
R3	2.2 MegΩ
R4	62 KΩ
C1	1 μF
C2	20 μF
C3	1500 pF

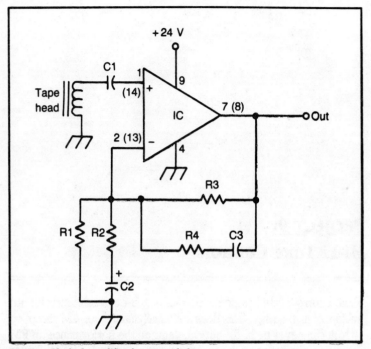

Fig. 8-1. Playback amplifier for a tape deck.

43

PROJECT 9:
Hi-Fi Tone Controls

Tone controls fitted to domestic radios and equivalent circuits are seldom of high quality. This does not usually matter for AM reception (which can never be hi-fi); but can degrade the performance on FM reception. Similar remarks apply to the tone controls fitted to lower priced record players and tape recorders.

High quality tone controls generally demand quite complex circuits. ICs enable the number of discrete components required to be substantially reduced and at the same time offer other advantages such as a high input impedance that matches a typical high impedance source. Tone control can also be combined with audio amplification in IC circuits.

Figure 9-1 shows a complete circuit based around a TCA8305 integrated circuit incorporating a feedback network which attenuates the low frequencies and boosts the high frequencies. (Parts list shown in Table 9-1.) At the same time, high frequencies can be attenuated by the treble control potentiometer at the input. The volume control, also on the input side, provides "loudness control" at both high and low frequencies to compensate for the loss of sensitivity of the human ear to such frequencies (i.e., both high and low frequencies tend to sound "less loud" to the ear).

A simpler circuit, using the same IC, is shown in Fig. 9-2, with parts list in Table 9-2. This has a single tone control potentiometer. The circuit provides flat response at middle frequencies (i.e., around 1 kHz), with marked boost and cut of up to ± 10 decibels at 110

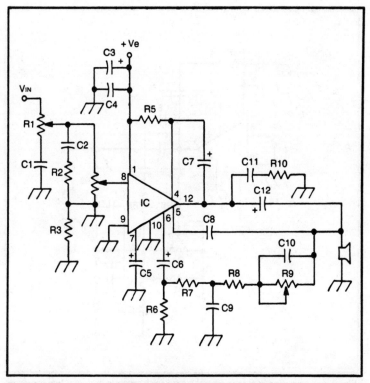

Fig. 9-l. Hi-fi tone control circuit suitable for receivers, record players and tape recorders and characterized by a high input impedance. Potentiometer R1 is the treble control. Potentiometer R9 is the bass control. Potentiometer R4 is the volume control.

Table 9-l. Parts List for Fig. 9-1.

R1	47 KΩ log pot	C1	47 nF
R2	10 KΩ	C2	820 pF
R3	1.8 KΩ	C3	100 μF
R4	100 KΩ log pot	C4	0.1 μF
R5	100 Ω	C5	100 μF
R6	15 Ω	C6	250 μF
R7	470 Ω	C7	100 μF
R8	470 Ω	C8	100 pF
R9	25 KΩ log pot	C9	0.33μF
R10	1 Ω	C10	0.22 μF
IC	TCA8305	C11	0.1 μF
		C12	1000 μF

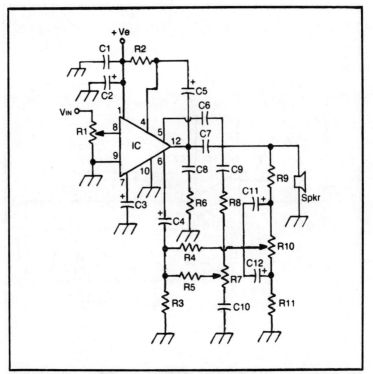

Fig. 9-2. Alternative hi-fi tone control circuit with separate high and low frequency feedback. Potentiometer R1 is the volume control. Potentiometer R7 is the treble control and potentiometer R10 the bass control.

Table 9-2. Parts List for Fig. 9-2.

R1	100 KΩ log pot	C1	0.1 μF
R2	100 Ω	C2	100 μF
R3	18 Ω	C3	100 μF
R4	180 Ω	C4	500 μF
R5	27 Ω	C5	100 μF
R6	1 Ω	C6	82 pF
R7	10 KΩ log pot	C7	1000 μF
R8	150 Ω	C8	0.1 μF
R9	330 Ω	C9	0.15 μF
R10	10 KΩ log pot	C10	2 μF
R11	15 Ω	C11	1 μF
IC	TCA8305	C12	2.2 μF

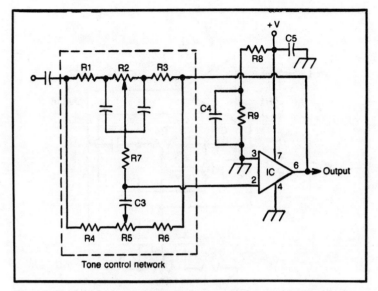

Fig. 9-3. Simple hi-fi tone control circuit. Component values are determined for a supply voltage of 32 volts. Potentiometer R2 is the bass control. Potentiometer R5 is the treble control. Components within the dashed outline comprise the tone control network.

Hz and 10 kHz respectively in the extreme positions of the potentiometer.

A (Baxandall) hi-fi tone control circuit associated with another type of op amp is shown in Fig. 9-3. (Parts list is in Table 9-3.) The IC in this case is the CA3140 BiMOS op amp. The tone control circuit is conventional and only a few additional discrete components are required to complete the amplifier circuit around the IC. This circuit

Table 9-3. Parts List for Fig. 9-3.

R1	240 KΩ	IC	CA3140
R2	5 MΩ log pot	C1	750 pF
R3	240 KΩ	C2	750 pF
R4	51 KΩ	C3	20 pF
R5	5 MΩ linear pot	C4	0.1 μF
R6	51 KΩ	C5	0.1 μF
R7	2.2 MΩ	Coupling Capacitor	
R8	2.2 MΩ	(C8) 0.047 μF	
R9	2.2 MΩ		

47

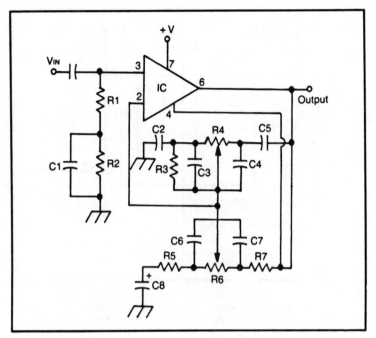

Fig. 9-4. Another hi-fi tone control circuit. Potentiometer R4 is the treble control.
Potentiometer R6 is the bass control. Supply voltage is 30 volts.

is capable of ± 15 decibels bass and treble boost and cut at 100 Hz
and 10 kHz respectively.

An alternative circuit using the same IC and giving a similar
performance is shown in Fig. 9-4, with the parts list shown in Table
9-4. Both of these circuits require a supply voltage of 30 to 32 volts.
Figure 9-5 shows the same circuit modified for dual supplies.

Table 9-4. Parts List for Fig. 9-4.

C1	0.1 μF	R1	5.1 mΩ
C2	0.01 μF	R2	2.2 MΩ
C3	100 pF	R3	18 KΩ
C4	100 pF	R4	200 KΩ linear pot
C5	0.001 μF	R5	10 KΩ
C6	2 μF	R6	1 MΩ log pot
C7	0.002 μF	R7	100 KΩ
C8	0.005 μF	IC	CA3140
		IC	CA3140

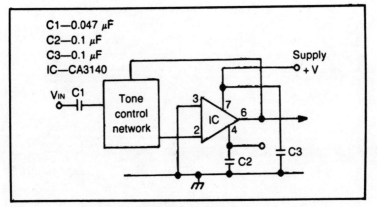

Fig. 9-5. Tone control for dual supplies.

PART II

For the Shop

PROJECT 10:
Constant Current or
Constant Voltage Source

A useful circuit employing the CA3018 integrated circuit array is shown in Fig. 10-l. This array comprises four transistors (two interconnected as a super-alpha pair) and four diodes. Tapping the super-alpha pair of transistors, a *constant current* source can be produced, the magnitude of this current being set by adjustment of the potentiometer R1 over a range of about 0.2 mA to 14 mA, depending on the actual supply voltage.

The same integrated circuit can also be used as a *constant voltage* source—Fig. 10-2. In this case, the constant voltage output is the zener voltage of the transistor that is worked as a zener diode, which is approximately 6 volts.

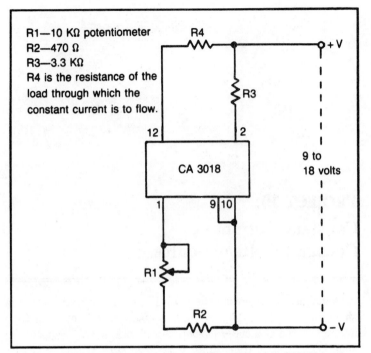

Fig. 10-1. *Constant current circuit using components found in CA3018 array.*

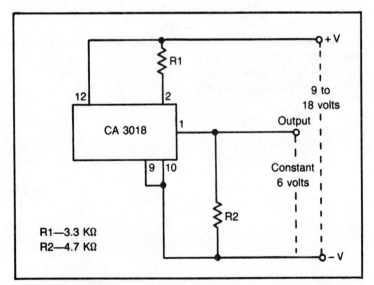

Fig. 10-2. *Circuit giving a constant 6 volts output from a 9- to 18-volt supply voltage, again using the CA3018 array.*

54

PROJECT 11:
Digital-to-Analog Converter

The parts and equipment that you will need to perform this series of experiments are listed in Table 11-1. The oscilloscope is optional.

The first thing you need to do is devise some source of a digital signal to convert into an analog voltage. The simple circuit shown in Fig. 11-1 will create a 4-bit work dependent on the position of the switches. If a given bit's switch is in the upper position, it will tap off approximately 5 volts from the voltage divider. This represents a logic 1.

Moving the switch to the lower position grounds out that bit. The output will be 0 volts, or logic 0. You can set the four switches to create any 4-bit binary word from 0000 to 1111.

The LEDs and their associated resistors are optional. If a given LED is lit, that bit is at logic 1. A dark LED implies a logic 0 output for that bit. The resistors are used to limit the current through each LED.

Three basic resistor values are used in this circuit. The resistor marked R_A should have a value of 33 K. The resistor marked R_B should have a value of 18 K. The resistors marked R_C may have values ranging from 220 to 470 ohms. A smaller value will cause the LED to glow more brightly. All R_C resistors should have the same value for a uniform display.

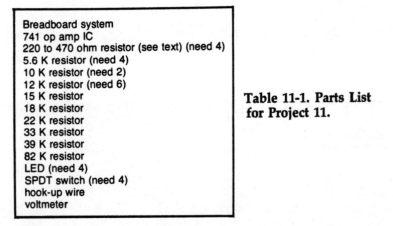

Table 11-1. Parts List for Project 11.

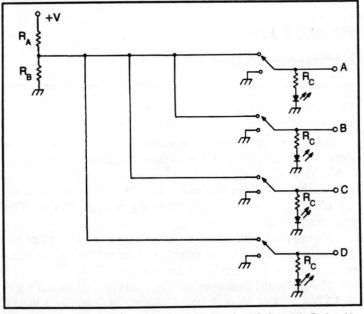

Fig. 11-1. This simple circuit can simulate 4-bit digital words for use in Project 11.

Breadboard the digital output simulator of Fig. 11-1 and the D/A converter circuit shown in Fig. 11-2. Use the following component values:

R1 = 82 K resistor   R4 = 10 K resistor
R2 = 39 K resistor   R5 = 10 K resistor
R3 = 22 K resistor   R6 = 15 K resistor

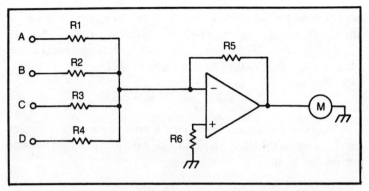

Fig. 11-2. This D/A converter circuit is explored in the first part of Project 11.

Bit A is the least significant bit (2^0, or 1). Bit D is the most significant bit (2^3, or 8). The 4-bit binary words will be written in the following order:

$$
\begin{aligned}
D\ C\ B\ A \\
1\ \ 0\ \ 1\ \ 1\ \ &= (1 \times 2^3) + (0 \times 2^2) + (1 \times 2^1) + (1 \times 2^0) \\
&= (1 \times 8) + (0 \times 4) + (1 \times 2) + (1 \times 1) \\
&= 8 + 0 + 2 + 1 \\
&= 11
\end{aligned}
$$

Any input bit at logic 0 will be feeding 0 volts into the input of the op amp. That bit will have no effect on the output. Set the binary switches for an input of 0000. The output should be zero volts (or very close to it).

Now raise the switch for input bit A, leaving the other three switches grounded. This makes the input word 0001. The D/A converter functions as an inverting amplifier with its gain set by the ratio of R5 and R1.

$$
G = -\frac{R5}{R1} = -\frac{10,000}{82,000} = -0.12
$$

The negative sign simply indicates that the output polarity is inverted. Because you will be using only positive input voltages in this application, the output always is negative.

The exact input voltage for a logic 1 input bit is set by the power supply voltage and the values of R_A and R_B in Fig. 11-1. Assuming the supply voltage is ± 15 volts, and R_A and R_B have the values specified earlier (33 K and 18 K respectively), this works out to approximately +5.3 volts. Component tolerances and variations in the supply voltage may cause slightly different values.

For an input of 0001, the output voltage should be equal to the input voltage (5.3 volts) times the gain (−0.12).

$$V_o = 5.3 \times -0.12 = -0.636$$

Measure the output. Do you get a value close to this? Return bit A to logic 0, and change bit B to logic 1 (0010). The input resistor for this bit is R2.

$$G = -\frac{R5}{R2} = -\frac{10,000}{39,000} = -0.26$$

Ideally this should be twice the gain of bit A ($2 \times -0.12 = -0.24$), but because you are probably using standard resistor values, you can be satisfied with coming close. Component tolerances cause deviation from the nominal values in any event. Once again, a logic 1 input bit equals 5.3 volts, so the output voltage for an input of 0010 is equal to V_{iG}.

$$V_o = 5.3 \times -0.26 = -1.36 \text{ volts}$$

Does the voltmeter read an output voltage close to this calculated value?

Ground bit B and raise bit C to logic 1 (5.3 volts). You should now have 0100 as your input binary work. The gain is set by R5 and R3.

$$G = -\frac{R5}{R3} = -\frac{10,000}{22,000} = -0.45$$

$$V_o = 5.3 \times -0.45 = -2.41 \text{ volts}$$

Next, set the input word to 1000. All switches are grounded (logic 0) except for D. What output voltage do you get now? It should work out according to the following equations:

$$G = -\frac{R5}{R4} = -\frac{10,000}{10,000} = -1$$

$$V_o = G \times D = -1 \times 5.3 = -5.3 \text{ volts}$$

What happens if more than one input bit is at logic 1? In this case, the circuit acts like a summing amplifier. The inputs are weighted by the different value input resistors. The output of this circuit is equal to the following relationship:

$$V_o = \left(V_{ia} \times \frac{-R5}{R1}\right) + \left(V_{ib} \times \frac{-R5}{R2}\right) + \left(V_{ic} \times \frac{-R5}{R3}\right) + \left(V_{id} \times \frac{-R5}{R4}\right)$$

For the component values you have been working with, the equation simplifies as shown here.

$$V_o = (V_{ia} \times -0.12)(V_{ib} \times -0.26) + (V_{ic} \times -0.45) + (V_{id} \times -1)$$

Set the input binary word to 0011. That is, A and B are each at logic 1 ($+5.3$ volts) and C and D are at logic 0 (0 volts). The output in this case should be simply the sum of A and B calculated separately. Plug the appropriate voltage values into the formula, and find the nominal output voltage.

$$
\begin{aligned}
V_o &= (5.3 \times -0.12) + (5.3 \times -0.26) + (0 \times -0.45) \\
&\quad + (0 \times -1) \\
&= -0.636 + -1.36 + 0 + 0 \\
&= -1.996
\end{aligned}
$$

For a 4-bit binary word, there are 16 possible combinations. Try the input to each combination and jot down your results in Table 11-2. Compare your results with the calculated values listed in Table 11-3.

For the next part of this experiment, you will use the R-2R ladder D/A converter circuit illustrated in Fig. 11-3. Again the input is obtained from the digital simulator circuit of Fig. 11-1. Use the following component values:

R1	12 K	R7	12 K
R2	12 K	R8	5.6 K
R3	22 K	R9	12 K
R4	5.6 K	R10	12K
R5	12 K	R11	5.6 K
R6	5.6 K		

The most significant bit ($D = 2^3 = 8$) passes through R1 and R2 before being fed into the inverting input of the op amp. The gain

Table 11-2. Worksheet for Project 11.

Input Word				Output Voltage	Input Word				Output Voltage
D	C	B	A		D	C	B	A	
0	0	0	0	_____	1	0	0	0	_____
0	0	0	1	_____	1	0	0	1	_____
0	0	1	0	_____	1	0	1	0	_____
0	0	1	1	_____	1	0	1	1	_____
0	1	0	0	_____	1	1	0	0	_____
0	1	0	1	_____	1	1	0	1	_____
0	1	1	0	_____	1	1	1	0	_____
0	1	1	1	_____	1	1	1	1	_____

for this bit depends on the ratio of R3 and R2 and the input voltage that passes through a voltage divider made up of R1, R4, R6, R8, and R10. The input voltage is tapped off at point E. The input signal passes through R1 and then is split off between R2 and ground through R4, R6, R8, and R10.

For a logic 0 input, the voltage at point E will simply be 0. For a logic 1 input, a 5.3-volt signal is fed through the voltage divider. The total resistance to ground is a sum of the resistances.

$$R_t = R1 + R4 + R6 + R8 + R10$$

$$= 12,000 + 5600 + 5600 + 5600 + 12,000$$

$$= 40,800 \text{ ohms}$$

According to Ohm's Law, the current flow should be equal to 0.13 mA.

Table 11-3. Calculated Values for Project 11.

Input Word				Output Voltage	Input Word				Output Voltage
D	C	B	A		D	C	B	A	
0	0	0	0	0.00	1	0	0	0	−5.29
0	0	0	1	−0.64	1	0	0	1	−5.94
0	0	1	0	−1.36	1	0	1	0	−6.65
0	0	1	1	−2.00	1	0	1	1	−7.30
0	1	0	0	−2.41	1	1	0	0	−7.70
0	1	0	1	−3.05	1	1	0	1	−8.35
0	1	1	0	−3.76	1	1	1	0	−9.06
0	1	1	1	−4.41	1	1	1	1	−9.70

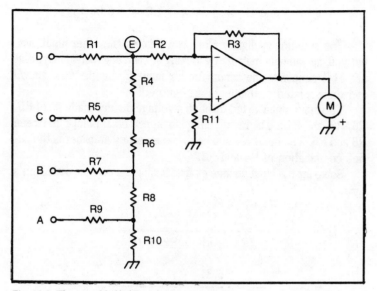

Fig. 11-3. *The second half of Project 11 examines the operation of a R-2R ladder type D/A converter.*

$$I = \frac{V_i}{R_t} = \frac{5.3}{40,800} = 0.0013 \text{ amp} = 0.13 \text{ mA}$$

The voltage drop across R1 equals 1.56 volts.

$$V_1 = I \bullet R1 = 0.00013 \times 12,000 = 1.56 \text{ volts}$$

Subtract this value from the original input voltage (5.3 volts.)

$$V_e = V_i - V_1 \times 5.3 - 1.56 = 3.74$$

This is fed into the inverting amplifier. The gain for the D input is calculated as follows:

$$G_D \frac{-R3}{R2} = \frac{-22,000}{12,000} = -1.8333 \cong -1.8$$

The negative sign simply indicates that the output polarity is reversed because the op amp's inverting input is being used.

The output voltage when input *D* is at logic 1 and the other three inputs are at logic 0 (1000) should be close to −6.86 volts.

$$V_o = V_E \times G_D = 3.74 \times -1.8 = -6.86 \text{ volts}$$

The situation is slightly more complex for the other input bits, but you can simplify matters by looking at each one individually. Figure 11-4 simplifies the schematic for input C. Inputs $A, B,$ and D and their related components are ignored.

The input signal is fed through a voltage divider made up of R5, R6, R8, and R10. The input voltage is tapped off at point F between R5 and R6. The input resistance to the inverting amplifier is the series combination of R4 and R2.

Solve for the input voltage by first finding the current with Ohm's Law.

$$I = \frac{V_i}{R_t} = \frac{V_i}{(R5 + R6 + R8 + R10)}$$

$$= \frac{5.3}{(12,000 + 5,600 + 5,600 + 12,000)}$$

$$= \frac{5.3}{35,200} = 0.00015 \text{ amp} = 0.15 \text{ mA}$$

$$V_F = V_i - V_C = V_i - IR5 = 5.3 - (0.00015 \times 12,000)$$

$$= 5.3 - 1.8 = 3.5 \text{ volts}$$

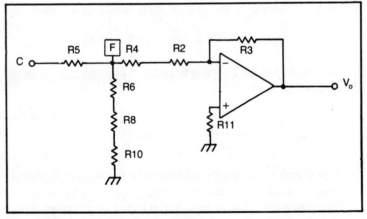

Fig. 11-4. Input C sees this equivalent circuit.

Next, find the gain for input C.

$$G_C = \frac{R3}{(R2 + R4)} = -\frac{22{,}000}{(12{,}000 + 5600)}$$

$$= -\frac{22{,}000}{17{,}600} = -1.25$$

So, the output voltage for $C = 1$ with the other bits $= 0$ (0100) works out to about -4.375 volts.

$$V_o = V_F \times G_C = 3.5 \times -1.25 = -4.375 \text{ volts}$$

Figure 11-5 shows the equivalent circuit for input B. Running through the equations for this input bit you find the following:

$$I = \frac{V_i}{R_t} = \frac{V_i}{(R7 + R8 + R10)} = \frac{5.3}{(12{,}000 + 5{,}600 + 12{,}000)}$$

$$= \frac{5.3}{29{,}600} = 0.00018 \text{ amp} = 0.18 \text{ mA}$$

$$V_g = V_i - V_B = V_i - IR7$$

$$= 5.3 - (0.00018 \times 12{,}000)$$

$$= 5.3 - 2.15$$

$$= 3.15$$

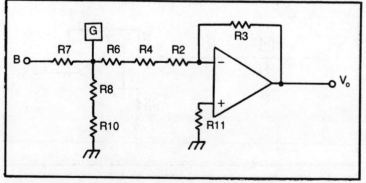

Fig. 11-5. This equivalent circuit is seen by input bit B.

$$G_B = -\frac{R3}{(R2+R4+R6)} = -\frac{22,000}{(12,000 + 5,600 + 5,600)}$$

$$= \frac{22,000}{23,200} = -0.95$$

$$V_o = V_G \times G_B = 3.15 \times -09.5 = 2.99 \text{ volts}$$

Finally, solve the equations for bit A. See Fig. 11-6.

$$I = \frac{V_i}{R_t} = \frac{V_i}{(R9+R10)} = \frac{5.3}{(12,000 + 12,000)}$$

$$= \frac{5.3}{24,000} = 0.00022 \text{ amp} = 0.22 \text{ mA}$$

$$V_h = V_i - V_A = V_i - IR9 = 5.3 - (0.00022 \times 12,000)$$

$$= 5.3 - 2.65 = 2.65 \text{ volts}$$

$$G_A = -\frac{R3}{(R2+R4+R6+R8)}$$

$$= -\frac{22,000}{(12,000 + 5600 + 5600 + 5600)}$$

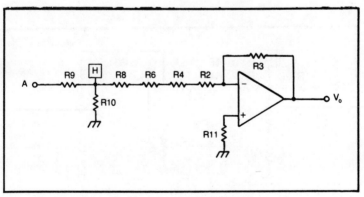

Fig. 11-6. Here is the equivalent circuit for input bit A.

$$= -\frac{22,000}{28,800} = -0.76$$

$$V_o = V_h \times G_A = 2.65 \times -0.76 = -2.02 \text{ volts}$$

Measure the output voltage for several combinations of digital inputs. There will be some imbalance of the steps because 12 K is not exactly twice 5.6 K, as required by the R-2R resistor network. For practical applications, low tolerance precision resistors should be used.

PROJECT 12:
Logic Probe

This project is a piece of test equipment that can be used to study and (if necessary) troubleshoot most of the projects presented in this book, and other digital circuits too. The project is called a logic probe. Logic probes are simple but powerful tools for analyzing what goes on in a digital electronics circuit. Many commercially available logic probes with all sorts of extra features can be readily purchased. However, this inexpensive do it-yourself logic probe will come in handy for any digital electronics experimenter. What this device lacks in special features, it more than makes up for with low cost. The project should not cost you more than two or three dollars.

A logic probe is simply a device that allows you to determine the logic state (0 or 1) at any point in a digital circuit. A super-simple two-component logic probe is shown in Fig. 12-1. The ground lead can be fitted with an alligator clip so that it can be connected to the same ground as that of the circuit being tested.

The probe is a short length of stiff solid wire, or use a common test lead probe. If this probe is touched to a point in the circuit with a logic 1 (high voltage) signal, the LED lights up. At all other times, the LED remains dark.

The resistor is used for current limiting. If the LED is allowed to draw too much current, it can be damaged. This resistor generally has a value of less than (1000 ohms), with 330 ohms being a typical value. This super-simple logic probe can be used without modification for any of the major logic families (CMOS, TTL or any of its

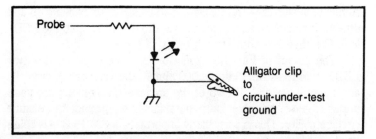

Fig. 12-1. *A super simple logic probe can be made from a resistor and an LED.*

variations, DTL, etc.). Because the circuit contains no active logic elements and takes its power from the circuit being tested, it is universal.

This circuit can be whipped together for under a dollar. While functional, this simple approach leaves a lot to be desired. For one thing, it does not give a definite indication of a logic 0 state. If the LED does not light, you could have a logic 0 signal, or the probe might not be making good contact with the pin being tested. There might even be a broken lead, or the LED itself could be damaged. With the circuit of Fig. 12-1, there is no way of telling.

Another potential problem area with this circuit is the possibility of excessively loading the IC output being tested. This can especially occur when the gate in question is already driving close to its maximum fan-out potential. Both of these problems can be side-stepped by adding a pair of inverters and a second LED/resistor combination, as illustrated in Fig. 12-2.

When a logic 0 is applied to the probe tip, the first inverter changes it to a logic 1, lighting LED A. The second inverter changes the signal back to a logic 0, so LED B remains dark. Conversely, when a logic 1 is fed into the probe tip, the output of the first inverter is a logic 0, so LED A stays dark, and LED B is lit up by the logic 1 signal appearing at the output of the second inverter.

This circuit can give a definite indication of either a logic 1 or a logic 0 signal. If neither LED lights up, the probe is not making proper contact. This circuit is much less ambiguous than the earlier version.

But that's not all this improved logic probe can tell you. This device can also indicate the presence of a pulsating signal (keeps reversing states). If the LEDs alternately blink on and off, a low frequency pulse is being fed to the probe. If both LEDs appear to be continuously lit, a high frequency pulse signal is indicated.

Actually, in this case the LEDs are still alternately blinking on and off, but it is happening far too fast for the eye to see, so the LEDs look like they are both staying on at all times.

The circuit of Fig. 12-2 calls for just five components—two LEDS, two resistors (330 to 1000 ohms—the value is not critical), and a hex inverter IC. Two of the six inverter sections are used in this circuit. The other four inputs should be grounded to ensure circuit stability. This is particularly important if a CMOS chip is being used.

Like the simpler version of the logic probe discussed earlier, this circuit steals its power from the circuit being tested. Alligator clips on the power supply leads can be attached to the power supply output of the circuit being tested.

A CMOS CD4009A hex inverter IC is the best choice, because it can be driven by either TTL or CMOS devices. By tapping into the tested circuit's power supply, the voltage levels will be automatically matched. In some cases, it might be desirable to add a pull-up resistor at the probe's input, as shown in Fig. 12-3. The value of this resistor is not critical, but it should probably be kept in the neighborhood of 1 K (1000 ohms).

If you intend to work with just TTL ICs, you can substitute a 7404 hex inverter (or the equivalent in the appropriate subfamily, like the low-power Schottky 74LS04). Use the pin numbers that are

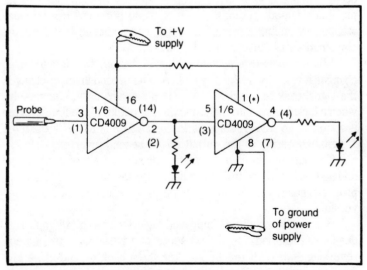

Fig. 12-2. An improved logic probe uses inverters to prevent circuit loading and to display both logic 1 and logic 0 signals.

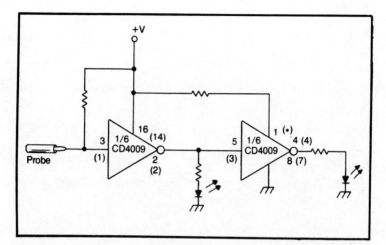

Fig. 12-3. If a pull-up resistor is included in your logic probe, a CMOS probe can be used on TTL circuits.

shown in parentheses in Fig. 12-2. This pin marked (*) has no equivalent on the 7404 and should simply be ignored.

I strongly recommend that you build a permanent version of this project. It will be useful throughout your project-building endeavors.

69

PROJECT 13:
Digital Capacitance Meter

Capacitance values can be readily measured over a wide range using digital ICs. The process is not all that different from the digital voltmeters described in the previous chapter. A basic digital capacitance meter circuit is shown in block diagram form in Fig. 13-1. The first stage is a monostable multivibrator. You should recall that a monostable multivibrator has one stable state. Assume the stable state is logic 0.

The output of the monostable multivibrator remains at logic 0 until the circuit is triggered. At that time, the output switches to logic 1 for a specific period of time that is defined by a resistor/capacitor combination. After this period of time, the output of the multivibrator returns to its stable state (logic 0).

In this application, the timing resistor is a fixed value. (In some cases, different resistors may be switch-selectable for different ranges.) The timing capacitor is the unknown capacitance being measured. Therefore, the output of the monostable multivibrator goes to logic 1 when triggered for a period of time that is directly proportional to the input capacitance.

The rest of the circuit is very similar to the digital voltmeters described in the last chapter. The output of the monostable multivibrator controls an AND gate that blocks or passes the reference oscillator signal through to the counter stage. The count is checked for over-range, decoded, and displayed.

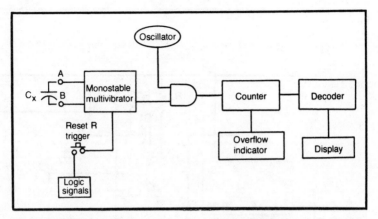

Fig. 13-1. A digital capacitance meter is quite similar to a digital voltmeter (Project 16).

Because the monostable multivibrator's on time is directly proportional to the unknown input capacitance, the count displayed will also be proportional to the value of C_x. A pushbutton to reset the counter and manually trigger the monostable multivibrator is usually mounted on the front panel of the instrument.

A practical capacitance meter circuit is illustrated in Fig. 13-4. The parts list is given in Table 13-1. Because the voltage across the test points (and therefore through) C_x is less than two volts, the measurement process is safe for virtually any component.

This unit is capable of measuring capacitances from less than 100 pF to well over 1000 μF. If electrolytic capacitors are to be tested, be sure to hook up the meter with the correct polarity. Point A should be attached to the capacitor's positive lead, and point B is negative. Resistor R1 sets the full scale reading for the meter. This component should be a trim pot that is set during calibration, then left alone. Once the necessary resistance is found, the trim pot could be replaced with an appropriate fixed resistor to eliminate the need for periodic recalibration. Smaller resistance values should be used to measure larger capacitances. A 100 K pot could be used for a 1X scale, while a 10X scale would be better served with a 5 K potentiometer. Multiple resistances could be set up for switch-selectable ranges.

USES FOR A CAPACITANCE METER

The obvious use for a digital capacitance meter is to determine the value of unmarked capacitors or to check to make sure a capaci-

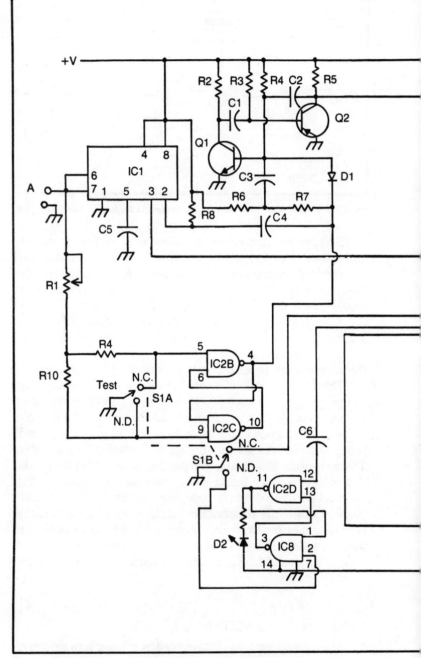

Fig. 13-2. The schematic for a complete digital capacitance meter.

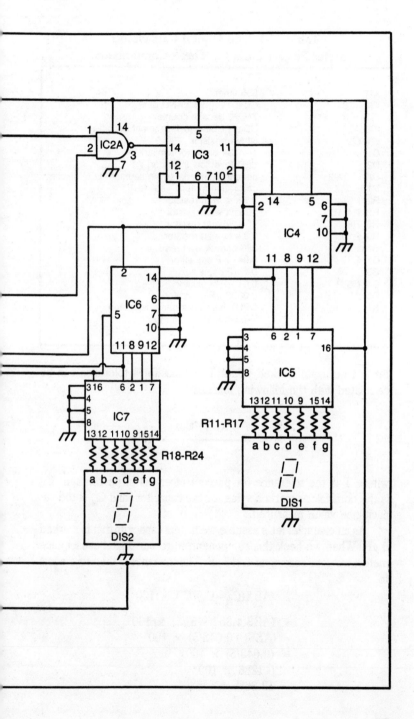

73

**Table 13-1. The Digital Capacitance
Meter Project Calls for These Components.**

IC1	555 timer
IC2, IC8	CD4011 quad NAND gate
IC3, IC4, IC6	74C90 decade counter
IC5, IC7	CD4511 BCD to 7-segment decoder
Q1, Q2	NPN transistor
D1	1N4734 diode (or similar)
D2	LED (overflow indicator)
DIS1, DIS2	common cathode seven segment LED display
R1	calibration trimpot—see text
R2, R5	2.7 k ¼ watt resistor
R3, R4, R7	15 k ¼ watt resistor
R6, R8	10 k ¼ watt resistor
R9, R10	1.8 k ¼ watt resistor
R11 - R24	330 ohm ¼ watt resistor
C1, C2	0.047 μF capacitor
C3	0.1 μF capacitor
C4, C5	0.01 μF capacitor
C6	0.0022 μF capacitor
S1	DPDT normally open pushbutton —push to clear and test

tor is true to its marked value. The capacitor's tolerance can be
calculated with the following formula:

$$T\% = \frac{ABS(C_M - C_N)}{C_N} \times 100$$

where T is the tolerance (or percent of error) in percentage, C_N
is the nominal, or marked value for the capacitor, and C_M is the capacitance value measured.

As an example, let's assume we have a capacitor that is marked
5 μF. When we hook this component up to our digital capacitance
meter, we get a reading of 4.357 μF. The tolerance is therefore equal
to

$$(ABX(C_M - C_N)/C_n) \times 100$$

$$= (ABS(4.357 - 5)/5) \times 100$$
$$= (ABS(-0.643/5) \times 100$$
$$= (0.643/5) \times 100$$
$$= 0.1286 \times 100$$
$$= 12.86\%$$

This is not bad for an electrolytic capacitor many of which often have rather wide tolerances, but it obviously would be a poor choice for any application requiring precision.

A digital capacitance meter can also be put to use in a number of other interesting ways. For instance, this type of instrument can come in handy for tracking down stray capacitances that can cause problems in many circuits, especially those operating at high frequencies. Printed circuit boards with closely placed traces are often subject to stray capacitance problems.

Components other than capacitors often exhibit internal capacitances that may need to be taken into account when designing precision circuits. For example, in an rf amplifier circuit, the transistor base-to-collector and emitter-to-collector capacitances can cause instability and/or oscillation in some cases.

Cables that consist of more than a single conductor have a natural capacitance per foot. These cables include coaxial cable, antenna twinlead, and ribbon cables. Because a capacitor is basically two conductors separated by an insulator, multi-line cables naturally behave as long capacitors.

The capacitance per foot of a cable can be determined by measuring a known length of the cable with a capacitance meter, and using the following formula:

$$C_f = \frac{C}{F}$$

where C_f is the cable's capacitance per foot, C is the measured capacitance, and F is the number of feet in the measured sample. C_f and C will always be in the same units. If C is measured in picofarads, C_f will also be in picofarads. Or, if C is in microfarads, C_f will be in microfarads too.

Let's say we have a 2 ½-foot sample of a cable. When you measure the capacitance of this length, you get a reading of 55 pF. Now, you can easily calculate the capacitance per foot. $C_f = C/F = 55/2.5 = 22$ pF per foot.

By rearranging this formula, you can determine the total capacitance of a length of cable if you know the capacitance per foot, and the length:

$$C_T = F \times C_F$$

where C_T is the total capacitance, F is the length in feet, and C_F is the capacitance per foot. As an example, assume you have a 235-foot length of the cable with the same capacitance as in the last example (22 pF per foot). The total capacitance works out to F × C_F = 235 × 22 = 5170 pF.

Another algebraic manipulation of this same formula allows us to determine how long an unknown length of cable is. This could be necessary if the cable is buried, embedded in a wall, or otherwise inaccessible for direct measurement. To perform the calculation, you need to know the capacitance per foot, and then take a reading of the cable's total capacitance. The formula is:

$$F = \frac{C_T}{C_F}$$

Let's say you need to determine an unknown length of a piece of the 22 pF per foot cable. Measure the total capacitance of the cable to get a reading of 4756 pF. The length of the cable is therefore equal to C_T/C_F = 4756/22—just over 216 feet, 2 inches.

Another novel application for a digital capacitance meter is as a digital thermometer. For this application, a high quality capacitor with a known temperature coefficient is needed. This specification is usually expressed as x parts per million per degree centigrade. For purposes of illustration, assume you have a capacitor with a wide temperature coefficient of 100 parts per million per degree centigrade. If this capacitor measures 0.1475 μF at 10 degrees centigrade, at 20 degrees centigrade it should produce a reading of 0.1465 μF. As you can see, a digital capacitance meter can be an extremely handy instrument to have on your workbench.

PROJECT 14:
Digital Frequency Meter

Most of the commercially available frequency counters around today use the "window" counting method. A sample of the input signal is allowed through a gate. This sample lasts a specific and fixed period of time. By counting the pulses during this sample period, the input frequency can be determined.

A block diagram for a "window" type digital frequency meter is shown in Fig. 14-1. The input signal is first fed through an amplifier stage to boost the signal to a usable level. An amplifier stage is not always used, but its presence improves the sensitivity of the instrument, allowing lower signal levels to be measured accurately.

The next stage of the circuit is a Schmitt trigger to convert any input waveshape to a rectangle wave that can be reliably recognized by the digital circuitry. If only square or rectangle waves are to be measured, the Schmitt trigger stage may be omitted. This processed input signal is fed to one input of an AND gate. The other input to the gating circuit comes from a reference oscillator, or timebase (as it is usually called in this application). The timebase feeds out three signals (or a single signal tapped off with delay circuits, as shown in the diagram). These three timebase signals are synchronized, and their timing relationship are critical. The three signals are illustrated in Fig. 14-2.

The first signal (labeled GATE) is fed to the input of the gating circuit, effectively opening (when logic 1) and closing (when logic

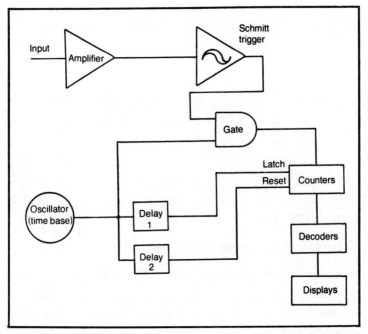

Fig. 14-1. *The basic digital frequency meter is another variation on the basic digital voltmeter.*

0) the "window," allowing the input pulses to be counted. The second signal, which is delayed until after the first is over, latches the output of the counters so they can hold their final value long enough to produce a readable display, while the third signal resets the counters to zero for the next measurement cycle. If the output latching was not done, the counter would count up to the appropriate amount, then immediately jump back to 000 and start over, never producing a stationary reading. With the latches, only the desired final count from each measured cycle is displayed.

Incidentally, the accuracy of most digital frequency counters is given as $x\%$ ± 1 digit. The least significant digit might bob up and down on successive measurement cycles. This happens because a partial input pulse can get through the "window," as illustrated in Fig. 14-3.

The timebase oscillator must be very precise in its output frequency with as little frequency drift as possible. Crystal oscillators are often used. The input frequency being measured must be higher than the reference frequency. If the input frequency is lower than the reference frequency, only 1 or 0 pulses can get through each

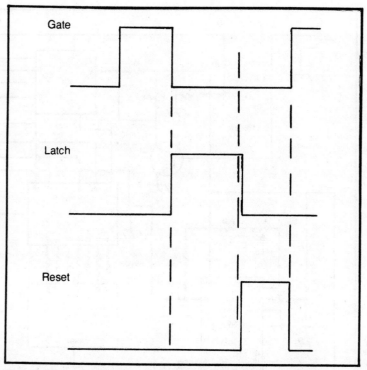

Fig. 14-2. Staggered pulses are required from the timebase oscillator in a digital frequency meter.

"window," which obviously would not result in a meaningful reading. To measure lower frequencies, an additional frequency multiplier input stage can be added between the Schmitt trigger and the gate. Similarly, to measure very high frequencies that would over-range the counter stages, a frequency divider stage could be added to drop the input signal to a lower frequency.

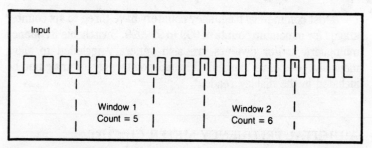

Fig. 14-3. Partial pulses appearing during the "window" counting time may cause some bobbing of the least significant digit.

79

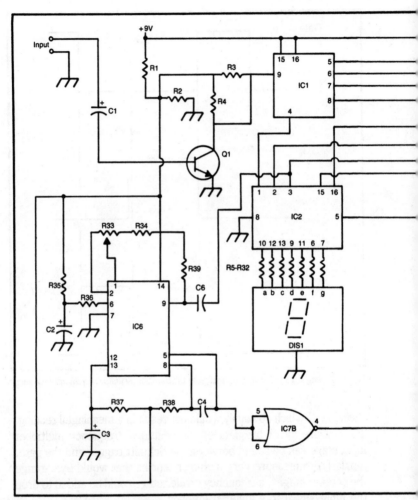

Fig. 14-4. A complete digital frequency meter is shown in this schematic.

Most commercial frequency counters have three to six counter stages for maximum counts of 999 to 999999. Switchable frequency multipliers and/or dividers are also generally included to allow manually selectable ranges. Decimal points may or may not be included in the display readout.

A DIGITAL FREQUENCY METER CIRCUIT

A complete digital frequency meter project is illustrated in Fig. 14-4. Table 14-2 is the parts list for this circuit. Each digit of the

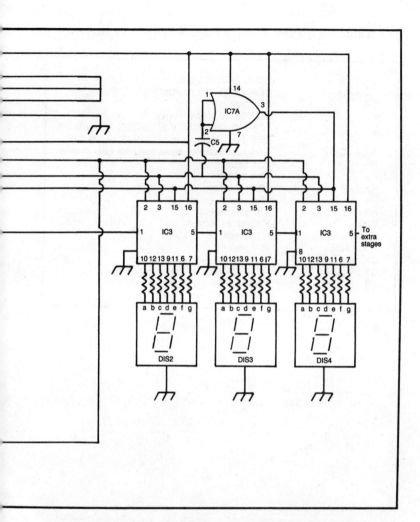

display is driven by a CD4026 decade counter (IC2 through IC5). Four digits are indicated in the diagram, but it is a simple matter to extend the display to contain additional digits. Simply connect pin 5 from the last stage to pin 1 of the following stage. The other pins of each IC are connected in the same way as for ICs 2 through 5.

Q1 and IC1 pre-condition the input signal so that it will have an acceptable level and waveshape to be reliably counted by the digital circuits. IC6 is wired as a reference oscillator, whose output frequency can be adjusted with R33, a 1MΩ trim pot. Calibration is done by applying a known frequency source to the input of the circuit and adjusting R33 for the correct reading.

Table 14-1. Parts List for Digital Frequency Meter.

IC1	14583 Schmitt trigger
IC2 - IC5	CD4026 decade counter
IC6	556 dual timer
IC7	CD4011 quad NAND gate
Q1	NPN transistor (2N3302, 2N5826, Motorola HEP-728, Radio Shack RS-2013, or similar)
DIS1 - DIS4	Common cathode seven-segment LED display
R1	22 k resistor
R2	18 k resistor
R3, R39	100 k resistor
R4	10 megohm resistor
R5 - R32	220 ohm resistor
R33	1 megohm trimpot
R34	470 k resistor
R35 - R38	10 k resistor
C1, C3	1 μF 35 volt electrolytic capacitor
C2	10 μF 35 volt electrolytic capacitor
C4, C5, C6	0.001 μF disc capacitor

PROJECT 15:
Multiple-Output Power Supply

This project can be used to power many of the experiments presented throughout this book. You can also use it to power other projects of your own. The circuit is shown in Fig. 15-1 and a parts list is given in Table 15-1.

Really, there isn't much to say about this circuit. There are 6 voltage outputs (with respect to ground):

+12 volts regulated	-5 volts
+9 volts	-9 volts
+5 volts regulated	-12 volts regulated

Notice that three of the outputs are directly regulated and should be almost exactly at their nominal values. The other three outputs are derived via resistive voltage dividers. Their values might be slightly off. Measure each of the outputs with a voltmeter. You might also want to check for output ripple with an oscilloscope.

Without heatsinking, each regulator should be able to supply about 0.5 amp without shutting down. Bear in mind that several outputs are taken off some of the regulators. The total current draw should not exceed 0.5 amp for each regulator. That is:

$$I_{+12V} + I_{+9V} = 0.5 \text{ amp}$$
$$I_{+5V} = 0.5 \text{ amp}$$
$$I_{-5V} + I_{-9V} + I_{-12V} = 0.5 \text{ amp}$$

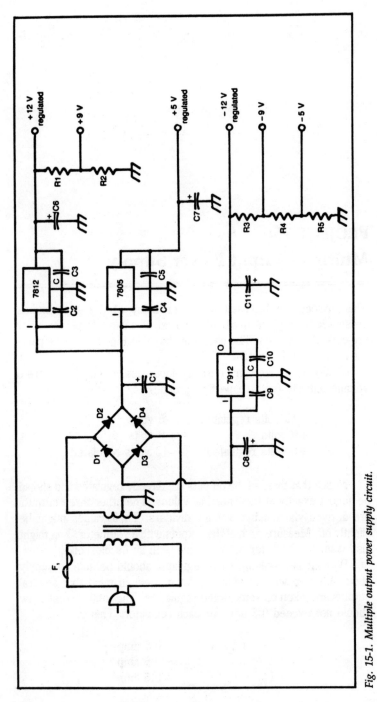

Fig. 15-1. Multiple output power supply circuit.

84

Table 15-1. Parts List for Multiple-Output Power Supply.

Voltmeter	
Oscilloscope (optional)	
1	ac line cord
1	36-volt, 3 amp transformer—center tapped
1	3-amp fuse & holder
1	7805 +5 volt regulator IC
1	7812 +12 volt regulator IC
1	7912 −12 volt regulator IC
D1-D4	1N4001 diode
C1, C8	500 μF 50 volt electrolytic capacitor
C2, C3, C4, C5, C9, C10	0.1 μF capacitor
C6, C7, C11	10 μF 25-volt electrolytic capacitor
R1, R3	2.2 K resistor (2200 ohms)
R2	6.8 K resistor (6800 ohms)
R4	2.7 K resistor (2700 ohms)
R5	3.9 K resistor (3900 ohms)

You can get greater output current by adding heatsinks to the regulators (you will need a heavier duty transformer and larger fuse too). Don't try to get more than one amp out of each regulator IC.

PROJECT 16:
Dc Voltmeter

In this experiment, you use an op amp to make a dc voltmeter. The parts and equipment you need are listed in Table 16-1.

Start by breadboarding the circuit shown in Fig. 16-1. Resistors R1 through R7 form a voltage divider network to provide a number of voltages to measure during the experiment. Use the following resistor values in the voltage divider:

R1	33 K	R5	22 K
R2	2.2 K	R6	10K
R3	10K	R7	33 K
R4	1 K		

The op amp is connected as a simple unity-gain non-inverting voltage follower with a voltmeter connected to the output. Connect the op amp's non-inverting input (V_i) to each of the points in the voltage divider network (labeled A through F). Write each measured voltage in the appropriate space in Table 16-2.

Compare your results to the calculated values listed in Table 16-2. Your measured voltages should be close to the ones listed here. There might be some deviation from the nominal values due to component tolerances op amp offsets, and minor measurement errors.

It's a simple matter to add gain to an op amp dc voltmeter simply by adding an input and a feedback resistor, as illustrated in Fig.

Breadboard system
741 op amp IC
1 K resistor (need 2)
2.2 K resistor
3.3 K resistor
4.7 K resistor
10 K resistor (need 4)
22 K resistor (need 2)
33 K resistor (need 2)
100 K resistor (need 3)
voltmeter (15 volt range)
hook-up wire

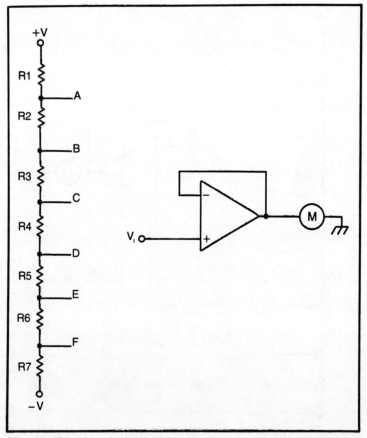

Fig. 16-1. This voltage divider network and unity gain dc voltmeter are used for the
first part of Project 16.

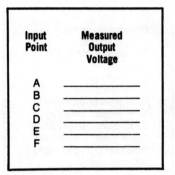

Input Point	Measured Output Voltage
A	
B	
C	
D	
E	
F	

Table 16-2. Worksheet for the First Part of Project 16.

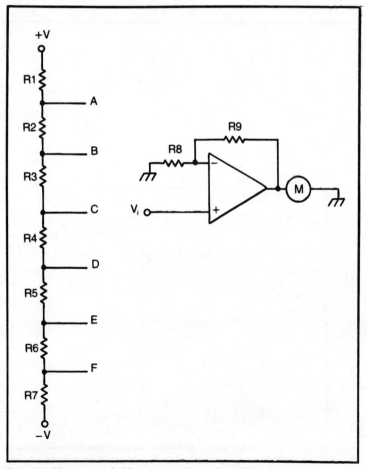

Fig. 16-2. *This project also demonstrates that a dc amplifier can have gain.*

Input Point	Calculated Output Voltage
A	+6.10 volts
B	+5.50 volts
C	+2.81 volts
D	+2.54 volts
E	−3.40 volts
F	−6.10 volts

Table 16-3. Calculated Values for the First Part of Project 16.

16-2. Remember to turn off the power supply while making changes to the circuit.

Use a 10 K resistor for R8 and a 4.7 K resistor for R9. Since this is a non-inverting amplifier circuit, the gain is as follows:

$$G = 1 + \frac{Rf}{R_i} = 1 + \frac{R9}{R8} = 1 + \frac{4700}{10,000}$$

$$= 1 + 0.47 = 1.47$$

Repeat the first part of the experiment, recording your values in the appropriate column in Table 16-4. Now change R9 to a 10 K resistor. Leave R8 alone. This makes the gain equal to Z.

$$G = 1 + \frac{10,000}{10,000} = 1 + 1 = 2$$

Table 16-4. Calculated Values for the Second Part of Project 16.

Input Point	Output Voltages		
	(R9 = 4.7 K)	(R9 = 10 K)	(R9 = 22 K)
A	___	___	___
B	___	___	___
C	___	___	___
D	___	___	___
E	___	___	___
F	___	___	___

Repeat the first part of the experiment, recording your values in the appropriate column in Table 16-4. Now change R9 to a 10 K resistor. Leave R8 alone. This makes the gain equal to Z.

$$G = 1 + \frac{22,000}{10,000} = 1 + 2.2 = 3.2$$

Repeat the measurements and record your results in the table. You might have found some of the measurements forced the op amp into saturation. This is to be expected. You must be careful not to exceed the op amp's maximum output voltage in using a practical dc voltmeter. Compare your results with the calculated values listed in Table 16-5.

A dc amplifier with gain is obviously most useful when the voltage to be measured is quite small. Small voltages may be difficult to measure directly.

Return to the circuit shown in Fig. 16-1. This time, use the following resistor values in the voltage divider:

R1	100K	R5	1 K
R2	1 K	R6	4.7K
R3	2.2 K	R7	100 K
R4	3.3 K	R7	100 K

Try measuring the tap-off points on the voltage divider using the unity gain dc voltmeter of Fig. 16-1. The analog voltmeter at the output should have a measurement range of about 15 volts.

Table 16-5. Worksheet for the Third Part of Project 16.

Input Point	Output Voltages		
	(R9 = 4.7 K)	(R9 = 10 K)	(R9 = 22 K)
A	+8.97 volts	+12.20 volts (*)	+19.52 (*)
B	+8.09 volts	+11.00 volts	+17.60 (*)
C	+4.13 volts	+5.62 volts	+8.99 volts
D	+3.73 volts	+5.08 volts	+8.13 volts
E	−5.00 volts	−6.80 volts	−10.88 volts
F	−8.97 volts	−12.20 volts *	−19.52 *

* The op amp may be driven into saturation, causing clipping of the output voltage.

Table 16-6. Measured Values for the Third Part of Project 16.

	Measured Output Voltages	
Input Point	Unity Gain	Gain = 11
A	_____	_____
B	_____	_____
C	_____	_____
D	_____	_____
E	_____	_____
F	_____	_____

Table 16-7. Calculated Values for the Third Part of Project 16.

	Measured Output Voltages	
Input Point	Unity Gain	Gain = 11
A	+0.86 volt	+9.46 volts
B	+0.72 volt	+7.92 volts
C	+0.41 volts	+4.51 volts
D	−0.06 volt	−0.62 volt
E	−0.20 volt	−2.18 volts
F	−0.86 volt	−9.46 volts

Record your results in Table 16-6. You will probably have some difficulty reading the meter. The differences will be slight, and the meter's pointer won't move very far.

Now use the dc voltmeter with gain shown in Fig. 16-2. Use a 10 K resistor for R8 and a 100 K resistor for R9. This gives the following gain:

$$G = 1 + \frac{100,000}{10,000} = 1 + 10 = 11$$

Measure the voltage at each of the tap-off points on the voltage divider and compare your results in Table 16-6. These voltages are easier to read, aren't they? Compare your measured voltages with the calculated values shown in Table 16-7.

In a practical dc voltmeter, you would draw a new scale to place on the meter face so that you could read the input voltage directly, even though it is being multiplied by the gain of the op amp.

Index

Index

Selected Index

Other Bestsellers From TAB

Other Bestsellers From TAB

Other Bestsellers From TAB